QUIT [BLEEPING] AROUND

77 Secrets to Superachieving

CHRISTINA M. EANES

Table of Contents

Introduction

To be yourself in a world that is constantly trying to make you something else is the greatest achievement.
—Ralph Waldo Emerson

This book is meant as a wake-up call for all who have allowed their light to dim. It's meant for those who no longer fully show up, because they are tired of light-dimming comments: "You are too happy" or perhaps "too productive"—"You're making us look bad." This is a call to action. It's time to quit [bleeping] around and become the superachiever that this world needs.

A superachiever is someone who gets things done. They are people who achieve whatever goals they set quickly and exceptionally well. The problem is that starting in early childhood, many of us superachievers allow others to dim our bright lights.

I have been a superachiever pretty much since birth. I started my own lemonade and golf-ball-sales business at age ten, strategically placing it on the ninth hole to increase sales and constructing a golf-ball retriever for the water hazard out of an old net and pole. From there I became a junior ski instructor and tennis instructor by age fifteen, and after graduating from college with honors, I quickly landed a high-paying management job. All of this was obtained while raising two children I intentionally had in college, so I could spend more time with them in their first couple of years and not have to worry about taking maternity leave in the professional world. I could go on and on about my life, but that's not why you're reading this.

I'm guessing this book attracted you because, like me, you've allowed your inner superachiever to lie dormant many times in your life, and you're tired of others telling you to quit thinking so big, slow down, and quit setting the bar too high. You've perhaps "laid low" to get a break from fighting the uphill battle you've fought most of your life.

Well, I'm here to tell you to stop it! Quit [bleeping] around, and unleash your inner superachiever. You must do what you were put on this earth to do—to leave it a better place than you found it.

I encourage you to use these seventy-seven secrets as motivation to unleash your true awesomeness. This is by no means an exhaustive list, but it should be a good start in inspiring you to get out of your own way.

The world needs you—it's time to quit [bleeping] around and get to it!

How to Read this Book

Some of the secrets build off of each other; however, for the most part, you can skip through and read the ones that you may need to "hear" at the moment. Each chapter contains a "Reflections" section to deepen your self-awareness for each secret.

Secret #1: Go Ahead...
Tell Me I Can't Do It!

Your attitude, not your aptitude, will determine your altitude.
—Zig Ziglar

"You can't do it." These words are motivation for a superachiever. They serve as a powerful inspiration to complete a task or achieve a goal.

My mother loves to tell the story of a grade-school incident in which a boy I was playing with said that I couldn't win against him in a swim race. He had a pool in his backyard and was a regular swimmer. I grew up in a mountain community, and at the time, we were visiting friends in "the lowlands." I could probably count on my fingers the number of times I had swam, but regardless, he ignited something in me, and I beat him in a swim race in his backyard pool.

The caveat here for superachievers is that we don't blindly respond to the taunt; it's got to be something we really want. I chose to become pregnant my second year of college (I married young) and, being a concerned parent, my father was worried and said that I wouldn't finish college. Because of his one comment, I vowed to get my doctorate. Within five years, I had earned a bachelor's and a master's degree. Ten years later, I started on my PhD and realized that I didn't really want it. It was simply a reaction to being told that I wouldn't finish college (now I have two master's degrees).

The lesson here for a superachiever is to have the mind-set that even when people don't believe in you, you must believe in yourself. You, and you alone, have the confidence in yourself and a level of self-awareness beyond the scope of others as to the true extent of your abilities.

Reflections

1. How does exceeding others' expectations of you motivate you?

2. Reflect on a time you were told you couldn't do something that you knew you could do. How did it feel when you succeeded?

3. Reflect on a time when you did something because you were told you couldn't, and you realized you didn't want to do it in the first place. What did you learn?

Secret #2: Adversity Really Is a Gift

All the adversity I've had in my life, all my troubles and obstacles, have strengthened me...You may not realize it when it happens, but a kick in the teeth may be the best thing in the world for you.
—Walt Disney

Superachievers see adversity as a gift and an amazing learning opportunity (although we don't always see this in the midst of our adversity—we are human, after all). Looking back, I've realized that all of my major growth has occurred when adversity was prevalent in my life.

My mother is an amazing woman. She was in her early twenties when she found out she was pregnant with me and soon found herself without the support of her first husband, who left her alone and destitute. Despite our struggles those first few years together, she always brought love and happiness into our lives. This rough beginning to life brought me the confidence that I can make it through anything.

My amazing father (i.e., stepfather), who came into our lives when I was five, passed away after battling cancer for a number of years. I learned to appreciate life more and to allow my inner superachiever out to play more often.

When I divorced my first husband, I became closer than ever to my children, and it opened the door for me to eventually meet a truly amazing equal partner in my life.

I could go on; however, you get the point. Adversity helps us dig deep within ourselves and realize what we're made of. It also helps us appreciate what we have, *and* gratitude is essential to being a superachiever.

Reflections

1. Tell the story of your life backward (starting from the present and working your way to the beginning). Make special notes of the times you faced adversity and how that path has led to who you are today.

2. Examine a particularly difficult time in your life, and list three gifts it has given you.

3. What does "What doesn't kill you makes you stronger" mean to you?

Secret #3: Must Be Resilient!

I am not what happened to me, I am what I choose to become.
—Carl Jung

Superachievers are resilient. Resilience is "the capacity to recover quickly from difficulties." This is all about how you look at hardship. Do you see it as something that makes you stronger or something that just happens to you, and you somehow need to survive it?

Being born to a remarkable woman who was in her early twenties, I learned a lot about resilience. At times, she had to work multiple jobs to feed and shelter the both of us. Whether we were living in a camper in someone's backyard or a coworker's attic, my mother continually created a nurturing environment to bring up her child.

Whether resilience is learned or you are born with it, it is key to not just surviving life but also thriving in life. Since superachievers are all about thriving, resilience is a very important aspect.

If you don't have a natural tendency to be resilient, how do you learn it? It is all about mind-set. Much like some of the other secrets presented in this book, it is about knowing and trusting that no matter what happens, you will make it through. It is about looking at problems as challenges to be overcome. It is about asking for help when you need it and accepting what is given to you. Ultimately, it is about having the self-confidence that you can conquer anything and be a better person as a superachiever because of it.

Reflections

1. How do you perceive the hardships that have occurred in your life?

2. What negative impacts have the hardships in your life had on you?

3. How are you a better person because of the hardships in your life?

Secret #4: A Word (or Two) about Fear

Everything you want is on the other side of fear.
—Jack Canfield

Superachievers do not allow our fears to paralyze us; rather, we use them to motivate us. The original purpose of fear was to allow us to either flee or prepare to fight in life-threatening situations, such as being stalked by a predator in caveman days. In modern-day society, in which we don't have to worry about natural selection as much, we've developed a few more responses to fear—the original fight or flight, along with freeze and freak out. Unfortunately, we've created so many stories in our heads about the dangers to us that we often resort to the last two.

Like many people, I initially had a fear of public speaking. I knew I would need to overcome it, because I dreamed of being a professional speaker one day. So I made it my mission to put myself in front of as many groups as possible, each time growing in my self-confidence. Now I relish every time I get to speak in front of a group.

The key is to think of fear as your friend—a messenger, if you will, on how important something is to you. When fear appears in your life, it means that you want to stretch yourself and to achieve something important to you. Your saboteurs, those negative voices in your head (Secret #16), don't want you to rock the boat. Following this train of thought, fear is something you want to experience, because it means that you are pushing yourself to stretch and grow and truly be a superachiever.

Reflections

1. Think of a time you allowed your fear to keep you from an opportunity. What did you learn from this?

2. Think of a time you overcame your fear. How did you feel?

3. What gifts has your fear given you?

Secret #5: Courage Is Not Optional

I learned that courage was not the absence of fear, but the triumph over it. The brave man is not he who does not feel afraid, but he who conquers that fear.

—Nelson Mandela

To be a superachiever, you must gather up all of the courage you can…and then muster even more. Superachieving is not for the faint of heart. To be a superachiever, you must take calculated risks, and to take risks, you must have courage—the courage to face circumstances and people who become obstacles in your path of superachieving.

Courage is simply the ability to do something that frightens you. There are varying degrees of courage. It can be anything from the courage to drive on the streets of New York City to the courage to be a part of a force that requires you put your life on the line every day to save others. Whatever level of courage is needed, the superachiever will utilize it to accomplish his or her goals and dreams.

It was not an easy decision to make, but I left behind a six-figure salary and a federal retirement to jump out into the unknown of being a small-business owner. Scary? Hell, yeah! Worth it? Totally. Even though I was excruciatingly scared of not having a safety net, I knew that it was what I was meant to do in my life, and I haven't looked back since. I knew that it wouldn't be an easy path, and I was OK with that, because as a superachiever, I don't like "easy." I want a challenge, and I want to leave an impact on this world—and that takes courage.

Reflections

1. How has your courage contributed to your current level of success?

2. What improvements can you make on your current level of courage?

3. What could you achieve with this new level of courage?

Secret #6: Determination. (Need I Say More?)

Determination gives you the resolve to keep going in spite of the roadblocks that lay before you.

—Denis Waitley

Once superachievers decide what we want, we dial in with a laser focus and don't give up until we've achieved our dreams. We enter into a state of flow (when the noise of the world falls away and time doesn't exist) and don't leave it until we've accomplished what we set out to do. This can be for goals that take ten minutes to dreams that take ten years to accomplish.

Not long ago, I participated in a leadership program that included a couple of days of ropes courses. One morning, the task we were asked to accomplish required working with a partner to climb what was affectionately termed as the "giant's ladder" and ring a bell at the top. The steps of the ladder were differing lengths apart, the average being about five feet. I was very excited about the challenge and was determined to reach the top with my partner. As we attached our harnesses to the ropes, I felt the determination rise up within me while the noise of the cheering fellow participants died away. It was just me, my partner, and the giant's ladder we were destined to conquer. We worked together with laser focus, and before I knew it, we were at the top of the ladder ringing the bell. As we rappelled down and unhooked our ropes, I noticed that I had multiple bruises starting to form on my arms and legs. I couldn't remember how I got them while working my way up the ladder.

Talent will only get you so far. Determination, a firmness of purpose or resoluteness whether you have the natural talent or not, will get you to the goal.

Reflections

1. How determined are you?

2. What are the positive aspects of your current level of determination? What about the negative aspects?

3. How can you supercharge your determination to get what you want in life?

Secret #7: Do Something That Scares You

If you realize that all things change, there is nothing you will hold on to. If you are not afraid of dying, there is nothing you cannot achieve.

—Lao Tzu

Perhaps you are asking, "Why on earth would I want to do something that scares me?" (Or you're thinking, "Hell yeah, what's next?") Doing something that scares you builds confidence; it helps you become more comfortable with risk taking, and it gives you something to visualize when you are afraid.

Back to that life-changing ropes course in the woods of North Carolina. I faced a lot of things that scared me; however, the ones that come to mind the most are those that required me to jump off ledges forty to seventy feet in the air. It was the scariest and most exhilarating thing I have done in my life up to that point. Speak to hundreds in an audience? No problem. Give birth to two kids with the assistance of only two Tylenol? Bring it. Jump off a sixty-foot ledge onto a zip line, or free fall (with a harness)? Holy crap!

Once you do something that really scares you, it helps you realize that you are unstoppable when you truly want something. Through this process, superachievers develop the courage to conquer their fears.

Also, in going through this process, you get to practice awareness of the body's natural reaction to fear and how you can overcome it. For example, I learned that I will not allow myself a lot of time to think about what I am about to do if it scares me. I now know that I need to distract myself until the moment I need to jump, and then I jump—I don't stand on the metaphorical ledge to give myself time to think about how scared I am of all the things that could happen. After all, isn't stress the unexperienced experience anyway?

Reflections

1. What really scares you?

2. What can you do to practice facing that fear?

3. What is your natural fear response, and how can you overcome it when you need to face something?

Secret #8: Get Over Yourself!

What we achieve inwardly will change outer reality.

—Plutarch

I know; it sounds a little harsh. However, we are our own worst enemies when it comes to getting in the way of our superachieving. Unequivocally, I would say if you haven't achieved something that you truly want, it is because you are getting in your own way.

There is a lot of mental stuff wrapped up in achieving. Common beliefs of superachievers can include "I'm too [insert descriptor here]; others won't accept me." I remember when just out of college, I became a manager in a professional field. I wasn't sure I would be accepted by the staff members, because most of them were older than me. My limiting belief was that I was too young and that they wouldn't listen to me. I decided that even though I had that concern, I would conduct myself as the best leader I could, and the outcome was that I was respected and loved in that position.

Drop the drama, excuses, and worries, and maintain a singular focus on your goal. Continually monitor your thoughts, and ask yourself if they are in honor of your highest self. If they are, that's great! If they aren't, stop thinking that way. It is quite simple—not easy but very simple. Only you control your thoughts. Find what thoughts you can use to replace those that aren't in your best interest. For example, I decided to replace the "I'm too young to be a good manager" with "I am an amazing leader, and my people love me."

Reflections

1. How are you getting in your own way?

2. What limiting beliefs are holding you back from superachieving?

3. For each belief, ask yourself, "Does this belief honor my highest self?" If not, release it.

Secret #9: What Do You Really Want?

You were put on this earth to achieve your greatest self, to live out your purpose, and to do it courageously.

—Dr. Steve Maraboli

Because superachievers excel at most things, it can be tough to decide what we want in life. It is essential to develop a set of criteria for yourself and use that as your tool to measure whatever you believe you really want as a goal or, ultimately, a dream.

In the eighth grade, I realized that I loved biology and thought I wanted to be a biologist when I grew up. I also had always been curious about law enforcement, but I knew I didn't want to be a police officer or a federal agent, so I never gave it a second thought. Once I got into college and started in my upper division biology courses in my junior year, I realized that being a biologist didn't really fit with my values, skill sets, and most of all, what got me excited about life.

I'll never forget the day this realization hit me—I was in the second week of classes, sitting in a biology lab, learning about what a Golgi apparatus was and why it was an important part of a cell. As I was sitting there, I realized that I could care less about what is inside of a cell and how DNA transcripts to RNA (or whatever it does). I gathered all of my things, left the lecture as the professor started on vacuoles, marched down to the admissions office, and transferred to the criminal justice department. I haven't looked back since!

In determining what you really want, look at what makes you happy. What makes your heart sing? What skills are you utilizing when you look up and three hours have passed in seemingly minutes? What are you doing when you realize you forgot to eat? If you're not sure yet, get a coach—they can help you work though all of this.

Reflections

1. Why were you put on this earth?

2. Where do most of your talents lie?

3. How can you express these skills and enthusiasm in a profession?

Secret #10: Nothing Can Stop You If You Truly Believe

You have the ability to choose which way you want to go. You have to believe great things are going to happen in your life. Do everything you can—prepare, pray, and achieve—to make it happen.

—Benjamin Carson

The key to superachieving is to believe deep down in yourself and believe in what you want to accomplish—to believe, without a doubt, that you can achieve what you want. I knew since childhood that I was destined to own my own business and that I would be successful at it. I took a bit of a detour, spending fifteen years in public service, and then decided that it was time; I could wait no longer (also thanks to my wonderful husband who was supportive of me going after my dream.)

In the past when I've questioned myself, it was an indicator that I needed to look at my goal or dream or myself more closely. If I questioned myself, I would seek what was behind the questioning. I would ask myself if it was really just fear, and if so, am I going to let it get in my way? If I questioned the goal or dream, I would examine whether or not it was something I really wanted.

When you completely believe without a doubt in your mind that you can accomplish your goal or dream, you position yourself, others, and your circumstances to move toward your goal or dream.

Reflections

1. Do you believe in yourself?

2. Do you believe in your biggest desire for yourself?

3. If your beliefs are holding you back, what can you do (or think) differently to move forward?

Secret #11: Be "Selfish"

To be successful you have to be selfish, or else you never achieve. And once you get to your highest self, then you have to be unselfish. Stay reachable. Stay in touch. Don't isolate.
—Michael Jordan

Being a daughter, mother, wife, leader, teacher, team member, and good friend, I've struggled with this concept my entire life until recently. As I get older (and wiser), I've come to understand that if I don't take care of myself or put myself first, then I'm no good to myself or others.

Embarrassingly, it has taken me many years to understand why I would put the oxygen mask on myself first before helping others on an airplane in the event of an emergency. If we don't take care of ourselves first, we will not be able to assist others.

Superachievers take care of ourselves. We understand when it is important to self-promote and take credit for a job well done. We often find ourselves saying no more than we say yes, to protect our very busy schedules and ensure that we are at our best for the challenges that we look forward to facing every day in our superachieving awesomeness.

As superachievers, we understand the Goldilocks principle. Remember the story *Goldilocks and the Three Bears*? Goldilocks kept trying porridge that was too hot, then too cold, then just right, and the beds that were too hard, too soft, and then just right. The same applies with being selfish. As superachievers, we take care of ourselves not too much and not too little—we are just the right amount of selfishness.

How do you know if you are just the right amount of selfishness? Let's look at self-promoting. If you talk about your accomplishments too little, you won't get that promotion at work you desire. If you talk about your accomplishments too much, people will find themselves counting how many times you say "I" and call you arrogant.

Reflections

1. What have you done for yourself lately?

2. What are your fears related to speaking up for yourself?

3. How can you be just the right amount of "selfishness" using the Goldilocks principle?

Secret #12: Overcome the Outshine Syndrome

If you set out to be liked, you would be prepared to compromise on anything at any time, and you would achieve nothing.
—Margaret Thatcher

There is a reason you stick out among your peers—superachievers are not average folks (I would venture to guess you are usually in the top one percent of whatever you do and definitely in the top 10 percent). The outshine syndrome occurs when you dim your awesomeness to help others feel better about themselves or so you can fit in with your social group better.

You are a superachiever! Others will feel bad about themselves around you because they can't keep up with you. In turn, some of them will try to knock you down a few pegs. I've struggled with this my entire life (with the exception of my middle school gifted program). If you can find other superachievers in your network, get to know them better and become each other's support system.

People seem to either support you as a superachiever and harness your gifts, or can't stand being around you because they feel inadequate. Develop an immunity to this; please don't struggle like many of us have.

My father shared a saying with me when I was a young child and was troubled that a best friend suddenly decided she didn't want to be friends anymore (I had won a costume contest that she believed she should have won). He told me, "Blowing out your candle won't make hers grow brighter." Since that time, I have heard a number of different versions of that saying and share it with as many young ladies as possible.

Don't dim your superachiever awesomeness! The human race needs the full wattage of your light to make this world a better place.

Reflections

1. How have you struggled with the outshine syndrome throughout your life?

2. In what areas of your life do you dim your light?

3. How are you going to increase your wattage?

Secret #13: Feedback Reveals a Lot about the Giver

What other people think about you has nothing to do with you and everything to do with them.

—Jen Sincero

What exactly is feedback? For our purposes, it is information people provide that they believe will either help you improve, or confirm what you are doing well. In other words, feedback comes from the viewpoints of others, based on their judgments, beliefs, opinions, and perceptions, or "JBOPs."

I struggled with this for a number of years. It all became clear when I attended a leadership program where we spent a full day giving each other feedback. As I watched everyone participate (being familiar with their frames of reference), I was able to observe and analyze the various exercises we completed. The main thing I noticed was that when people were providing a critique (myself included), it was generally something they wished for themselves. For example, one individual said that the feedback recipient needed to step into her power more, which was actually a struggle of the person giving the feedback.

Looking back through the years, much of the feedback I have been given would have held me back if I had acted on it. Feedback such as "Don't smile so much in meetings" or "Slow down, you're producing too many reports" attacked who I fundamentally was (and was more revealing of the unhappy person or the individual who couldn't keep up with me.)

Knowing that the feedback you receive is more indicative of the giver, it is still important to ask yourself, "What is the 2 percent truth that I can learn from this?" It is essential to consider your impact on others *and* to not let your concern with feedback hold you back from superachieving.

Reflections

1. Is there a certain theme to the feedback you've been given throughout your life?

2. What does the feedback tell you about the giver?

3. What is the 2 percent truth you can learn from it?

Secret #14: Seek Internal Fulfillment

Success is about enjoying what you have and where you are, while pursuing achievable goals.

—Bo Bennett

This is a big one for superachievers—it is easy to get addicted to achieving and allow it to become a part of your identity. The problem then becomes that you continue going after bigger and bigger wins to get the next accolade, and before you know it, you're accomplishing goals you had no intention of pursuing in the first place.

It can be a fine line between superachieving and crossing the line into the "I'll be happy when..." syndrome. If you find yourself saying that you'll be happy when you get that promotion, or that degree, or win that event, then it's time to stop and reflect on what's going on within.

Fulfillment is satisfaction or happiness as a result of fully developing one's ability or character. If you seek internal fulfillment, you will realize that you are happy with who you are, and you go after your dreams because the process of achieving dreams brings you great joy. It is all about the journey, not the destination (Secret #77). This is a totally different mind-set, one that puts you more into a relaxed Zen way of being, versus an anxiety-ridden way of being. In order to truly superachieve, you need to be more in a "chilled" state of mind, as it allows you to accomplish so much more without totally burning out your body and mind in the process.

Reflections

1. How do you feel when you receive recognition for your accomplishments?

2. How do you feel when you do not receive recognition for your accomplishments?

3. If you don't feel the same, how can you feel just as good about your accomplishments with or without recognition?

Secret #15: Toot Your Own Horn!

As I've said before, and by gosh, I'll say it again—don't be afraid to toot your own horn.

—Emlyn Chand

So many of us have trouble singing our own praises when we really should, especially us superachievers of the female persuasion. Maybe it is our upbringing, or maybe it is society, but the *why* doesn't matter.

Being a superachiever means strategically placing yourself in positions that help you to achieve your goals. In order to do this, you need to connect with others in positions that can help you and be able to show them what you are capable of. You can't do that if you are constantly eating humble pie and not promoting yourself.

I had difficulty self-promoting at first; however, I quickly learned that this is key in positioning oneself to accomplish goals. This doesn't mean that you forsake partaking all humble pie; it just means that you balance giving others credit with giving yourself credit. For example, when I was a manager speaking to my team, I would use lots of "we" language and recognize those team members that went above and beyond to accomplish the mission. Then when I would report up the chain of command, I would still recognize the efforts of my team members; however, I would emphasize how all of this great work was done under my leadership. Even if you aren't in an official leadership position, you can still sing the praises of your team while emphasizing how your contributions were vital to the team's success.

There are two areas of caution: (1) be careful not to overuse "I"—make sure there is a nice balance between "I" and "we," and (2) never, ever, ever, try to put someone else down to make yourself look better. Not only is this just wrong, but it will also burn a lot of bridges.

Reflections

1. Reflect on whether you promote yourself enough to the people who can help you along your superachiever journey.

2. Identify key individuals that can help you in accomplishing your goals.

3. How can you promote yourself more with each of these individuals?

Secret #16: Don't Listen to the Negative Voices!

Stress and unhappiness are always a choice. Any negative feelings you experience are because you've chosen to listen to your saboteurs.

—Shirzad Chamine

Let's talk about the voices in your head. We all have them (some more than others). However, most of us are not aware of them...until we intentionally bring awareness to them. The mind is meant to be our servant, a tool to help us accomplish what we were put on this earth to do, but it often turns into our master. You are not your thoughts—at least not most of them.

Since birth, our minds have recorded everything that has occurred in our lives. We couldn't function if we were consciously aware of all of these memories. So we have a subconscious and a conscious, and we only operate in our conscious mind anywhere from 5 to 10 percent of the time (depending on which studies you review). This means that 90 to 95 percent of the time, you are operating out of your subconscious (i.e., purely reacting to stimuli, rather than responding.)

In the coaching world, we use the words "saboteur" or "gremlin" to describe the subprogramming that can get in your way. The more you are aware of it, the better you will be able to respond when you are triggered rather than reacting based on your past programming.

You know when a saboteur or gremlin has reared its ugly head, because you feel triggered. For example, you are speaking in front of a group, and someone rolls his or her eyes. If you take it personally, you have been triggered (you'll feel a response in your body, and an emotion will arise). If you have a saboteur in this area, you'll hear a voice that will say something such as, "Why does this always happen to me?" or "How dare that person do that—*what a jerk!*" Superachievers are aware of these voices and do not let them get in the way of our superachieving.

Reflections

1. Go to www.positiveintelligence.com/assessments, and take the saboteur assessment. Carefully read through it, and identify your top three.

2. Reflect on when your saboteurs get activated and the types of things they say to you as they show up in your thoughts.

3. Come up with a game plan for having a greater awareness of your saboteurs (*Positive Intelligence* by Shirzad Chamine and *Taming Your Gremlin* by Rick Carson are great books to read on this topic).

Secret #17: Got Metacognition?

Without reflection, we go blindly on our way, creating more unintended consequences, and failing to achieve anything useful.
—Margaret J. Wheatley

A trap that many superachievers fall into is to keep going and going, like the Energizer bunny, pursuing our goals/dreams. But when something isn't working, we start analyzing the problems that have arisen as though they're a puzzle to be solved, because our minds work so quickly. We often neglect to stop and think about *how* we think, which is also known as "metacognition."

A great model, developed by Chris Argyris and Robert Putnam, can help superachievers boost their superachieverness. The OAR model (observer-action-results) indicates that we, as the observers, take in data (through one or more of our five senses), and then we take action and get results. When we don't get the results we want, we generally have three different reactions:

1. We do nothing, assuming the results we got are out of our control. For example, I didn't get the promotion because my boss just doesn't like me.
2. We go back and try all kinds of different actions to get different results until we succeed.
3. We go back and analyze the observer. How did our thoughts/beliefs get the results we experienced?

The third response is the most powerful for a superachiever. We need to be keenly aware of how our thought processes work and how they contribute to our successes or failures (i.e., learning experiences). This is also why we like to surround ourselves with people who think differently than we do. It may be difficult to communicate with them at times, but they are tremendous resources when we need to expand our frames of reference.

Reflections

1. Think back to a recent time when you didn't achieve the results you wanted. Which of the three potential responses did you have?

2. How did your thinking get you those results?

3. How could you have adjusted your thinking to achieve different results?

Secret #18: Is Your Vision Crystal Clear?

One reason so few of us achieve what we truly want is that we never direct our focus; we never concentrate our power. Most people dabble their way through life, never deciding to master anything in particular.

—Tony Robbins

This is a huge one. As a superachiever, it's something I've always known but not consciously until recently. Once you identify what you want to achieve, you must set a crystal clear vision of what you intend to occur. Visualize yourself accomplishing your goal. Include a detailed scene of you celebrating the achievements of your goal, one that involves all five senses and your emotions. The brain doesn't know the difference between a detailed visualization and real life; you'll feel it so deeply, and you'll believe it so deeply, that the only thing left to do is to actually accomplish it.

I've always naturally done this, but the necessity of it became quite evident in a recent leadership retreat program I participated in. One day involved a number of what I felt were death-defying high ropes challenges. One of the challenges was lovingly called the "pamper pole," because people who made it to the top would need to wear diapers. The goals of the exercise were to climb to the top of the pole, stand up on it (as it swayed), and then jump off to hit a ball hanging above and out about ten feet from the pole.

The seemingly one-hundred-foot pole (I'm sure it was more like thirty to forty feet) scared the bejeezus out of me. So, being a superachiever, I raised my hand to go first. I climbed to the top of the pole, struggling as it began swaying. I then fell off as I attempted to get both of my feet onto the top of the pole. After the adrenaline rush subsided, I realized that I had never set the intention of standing up on the pole; I had only envisioned making it to the top. And that, my friends, is the power of intention!

Reflections

1. Reflect on the process you use when setting a goal. Do you include an intention?

2. How do you set an intention? Or if you don't, how will you set an intention now?

3. How can you make that intention crystal clear, involving all five senses and your emotions?

Secret #19: Dream Big...
Then Even Bigger!

To achieve the impossible, it is precisely the unthinkable that must be thought.

—Tony Robbins

I used to say "the sky is the limit," but now I don't like being limited that much. Whatever saying you like to use to motivate yourself in dreaming big—use it! This is key to being a superachiever and can be hard for the average person to do. The reason this can be hard is that the mind can get in the way during the process, with fear and all kinds of excuses on how [insert big dream here] won't work.

In order for you to accomplish the impossible, you have to be able to dream the impossible and have almost an irrational belief that you can accomplish it. (More on this in Secret #66: I can do it!) Many things in my life started out as almost impossible dreams, including the idea of going to college; however, I continue to surpass them all.

My big dream of being an author and speaking to thousands in an audience is so close I can almost taste it, and I'm already working on ways I can make the dream bigger. It is quite a simple process—think about the biggest dream for yourself, and figure out how you can stretch it even more. Once you find yourself getting closer to it, stretch it even a bit more. For example, my initial dream was to speak to a group of five hundred (before that, I had only spoken to much smaller groups). Once I got close to five hundred, I increased the goal to speak to over one thousand. Even though I haven't reached that one yet, I've already set a goal for ten thousand. That is just what we do as superachievers—we continually find ways to stretch ourselves out of our comfort zones, because that is where growth happens.

Reflections

1. What is your process in dreaming big?

2. What is your biggest dream for yourself right now?

3. How can you make it bigger?

Secret #20: Make Sure It Really Is Your Dream

Happiness will never be achieved by chasing someone else's dream. Make sure the ones you're chasing are yours.
—Unknown

This can be tough for superachievers, because we are truly driven to achieve. It is an internal push that we continue to set goals and achieve them. If you don't take the time to really figure out what you want for your life, then you may well be going after someone else's dream simply to keep achieving.

I idolized my father as a child, because he was an amazing man and a superachiever himself. Bless his soul; if I would have chosen to live the dream he had for me, I would have had a full-ride college scholarship for tennis and then become a K–12 teacher. I was well on my way to accomplishing these dreams until I decided at seventeen that was not what I really wanted for my life.

There is also a certain amount of guilt involved when you let someone else down, especially a parent. I was lucky in that my father's ultimate dream was for me to be happy, so he was supportive of me in whatever I chose to do. You may not be so lucky. Regardless of the disappointment of others, especially those who hold a prominent place in your life, you *must* follow your own dreams. You were put on this earth to fulfill a purpose, and only you truly know what that is, not someone else. When I say *know*, I mean either consciously or subconsciously. If you don't consciously *know*—get some coaching. It is amazing how much clarity one-on-one development can bring to a superachiever. We'll cover more of this in Secret #57.

Reflections

1. Who or what has influenced your dreams?

2. Really examine your dreams—are they yours?

3. What is your life purpose? Is it reflected in your dreams?

Secret #21: Compete with Yourself Instead of Others

A flower does not think of competing to the flower next to it. It just blooms.

—Unknown

For the superachiever, it is not about winning against others; it is about competing with one's own self. The superachiever high comes when you've finally conquered whatever was holding you back from achieving the goal or dream. Of course, superachievers can appear very competitive to others. It is true that we utilize others as benchmarks in our competitiveness with ourselves, which could indeed give the appearance of a supercompetitor.

This was never clearer than when I was fourteen years old, in middle school, and excited to have qualified as the number-two singles player on the high school varsity tennis team. I decided that my goal was to become the top player on the team by the end of the school year; I wanted to enter my high school years being number one on the team. Naturally, the number-one player on the team became my benchmark for how I measured my improvement throughout the year. At the beginning of the year, she would win our matches without even giving me a game. (If you're not familiar with high school tennis scoring, a match generally consists of two sets, with each set requiring a player to win six games to win a set—there's much more to it, but you get the gist).

This motivated me to work my butt off the entire year, and by the end of the year, I beat her in the district finals and went on to take third in the state high school championships. People commented on how competitive I was with her the whole year, but what they didn't understand is that it had nothing to do with her. She was my benchmark for measuring both my progress and the accomplishment of my goal to become a tennis player at a certain level.

As a superachiever, it is good to be aware of others' perceptions of you; however, do not let them change how you go after your goal or dream. As long as you are ensuring that you are competing with yourself, you will soar quicker than ever before.

Reflections

1. What are your views on competition?

2. How have you utilized others to benchmark your achievements?

3. Describe your superachiever high—the feeling you get when you've achieved your goal or even your dream.

Secret #22: Ensure Your Head, Heart, and Gut Are Aligned

If my mind can conceive it, and my heart can believe it, I know I can achieve it.

—Jesse Jackson

Too often, as humans, we solely rely on our minds to decide our goals and dreams. When we do, we're leaving two very important neural centers out of the process. Interestingly, there are three neural centers in the body—the brain, the heart, and the gut areas. If we are really in tune with our thoughts, feelings, and bodies, we know when these are out of whack.

For example, when you make a purely logical decision, you may feel a tightening in the chest along with an emotion and gut feeling of doubt. This means that you aren't in alignment. Or you can make a decision of the heart—"I really love him or her"—while the gut is telling you, "danger, danger," and the brain seems to have stepped out of the picture completely.

I won't go into all of the science behind this—feel free to research it if you'd like. Or why not simply check with your head, heart, and gut on how they feel about it?

As a superachiever, anytime you make a decision to focus all your energy and amazing talents on achieving a particular goal or dream, it is important to make sure you are completely on board with it—mind, heart, and gut.

Reflections

1. Reflect on a decision you've made in the past that didn't turn out so well. What was the main neural center involved in the decision-making process?

2. How do you know when you are involving your head, heart, and gut in a decision?

3. Develop a "check-in" process for when you are making a big decision to involve all three of your neural centers.

Secret #23: Get a Fan Club

I've got a lot of dreams I want to achieve, and I hope someone can cheer me on as I'll cheer them on in their dreams.

—Hunter Hayes

Behind every superachiever is a fan club, individuals that support you as you take on the world and help lift you up when you face the inevitable disappointments along your journey. (Obviously, this isn't a one-way street; you're just as supportive of them as they are of you.)

Some superachievers try to go it alone, thinking that others hold them back. We only get so many trips around the sun in this life, and it really is all about the journey. Without a team of loved ones to journey with you, it can certainly be lonely and less fulfilling.

This team of loved ones can be made up of family members, but it doesn't have to be. They are people you have chosen to include in your life that bring you joy and love and help you surge forward toward your dreams, never holding you back. This *is* essential. If someone in your life is constantly criticizing you or belittling you, it is time to limit your exposure to them.

One measure I've used throughout my life is "Am I better with them or without them?" Think of this as both an internal and external measure—am I physically, socially, and financially better off without them? *And* am I a better person—my best self around them—or am I my worst self around them?

In the latter years of my first marriage (I married very young, as mentioned earlier), I realized I couldn't be who I was meant to be in that relationship. Because my first husband and I were from completely different backgrounds and had grown to be quite different people, I held back who I was and judged him for being who he was. I had grown to not like who I was around him, and we were not true partners in our marriage. We parted ways, and now we are much happier with more compatible partners. I since have soared into superachiever awesomeness with a supportive, loving, and very compatible partner, because I can be myself every day, without apology.

Reflections

1. Who is in your fan club?

2. Who in your fan club helps you be a better person?

3. Is there anyone whom you should limit your exposure to because you are your worst self when that person is around?

Secret #24: Problems Suck. Challenges Rule!

We can't solve problems by using the same kind of thinking we used when creating them.

—Albert Einstein

Superachievers don't have problems—we have challenges. It is truly all about how you look at it, your perception.

Think about it...

A problem is something that drains your energy, something that weighs heavily on your "to do" list to solve, and something you spend endless hours worrying and complaining to your confidants about.

A challenge is something that creates energy and something that leads you to say "Hell, yeah!" You dive in to meet the challenge head on while your fan club cheers for you from the sidelines.

Do you see the difference in the energy behind each of these? One is heavy and dark, while the other is light and motivating.

Superachievers don't have problems. Rather, we see them as challenges and opportunities to demonstrate our amazingness. It may be external, such as coming up with a new process or procedure at work because the old one didn't work, or internal, such as figuring out how to positively experience a bad boss and learn from the experience rather than letting it stress us out.

Reflections

1. What is your perception of a problem versus a challenge?

2. How can you change your perspective to see *all* of your problems as challenges?

3. If you could adopt this perspective, how would it change your life?

Secret #25: Enlighten Me!

Everything that irritates us about others can lead us to an understanding of ourselves.

—Carl Jung

Enlighten Me! is a very simple yet profound technique to manipulate your perception and bring you even further into superachieverhood. Quite simply, it is pretending that everyone else is enlightened, you're not, and you want to learn how to be enlightened (obviously—you're a superachiever).

How it works is that you ask yourself, "What is this person teaching me right now?" when in contact with others. This can literally be done every time you are in the presence of another human being.

For example, I was in line at a grocery store recently and started getting frustrated because the clerk and the customer ahead of me were chatting it up as if they didn't have a care in the world. I remembered that I needed to practice what I preach and asked myself what they were teaching me in that moment. I realized that they were demonstrating how important it is to connect with others, to stop and smell the roses, and to have patience—all lessons I have trouble with as a superachiever, because I'm all about action and go, go, go.

As superachievers, we look at each moment in our lives as an opportunity to grow and further develop into the people we want to be.

Reflections

1. Think back to a recent situation when you felt frustrated with an individual—either someone in your life or just in passing. What was that person teaching you?

2. How can using the *Enlighten Me!* method change your perception?

3. How will you implement this method in your life?

Secret #26: Get a Reality Check

Whatever we plant in our subconscious mind and nourish with repetition and emotion will one day become a reality.
—Earl Nightingale

As humans, we literally create our own reality. Good or bad, we make up stories about everything we experience. With his Ladder of Inference, Argyris breaks down exactly how we form our stories:

1. In the first step, an "event" occurs. For example, I provide an update to my boss in front of my team members, and she tilts her head, frowns, and asks me a question.
2. The next step is that we select "data" from that event. The data I selected was the head tilt, the frown, and the asking of a question.
3. We then add meaning to that data. The meaning I added was that my boss was really asking me, "What were you *thinking*?"
4. Next, we make assumptions based on the meaning we added. The assumption I made was that she didn't think I was taking the project in the right direction.
5. We then form conclusions. The conclusion I formed was that she thought I wasn't qualified for my position.
6. These conclusions become beliefs. I then began to *believe* that she didn't feel I was qualified for my position.
7. We then act on these beliefs. Having this belief, I avoided her and did my best to stay under her radar.

Knowing that we do this, it is important that as superachievers, we constantly "reality check" ourselves by asking, "Is this story I created in my best interest?" In the example I provided, that story was not in my best interest, so I investigated it by talking to several people, reviewed my thinking process, and decided to change it.

Even if my boss thought I was incompetent (it turns out she thought I was a valuable member of her management team), I could have tweaked my story to be more beneficial—instead of seeing her "perspective" of me as a problem, I could see it as a challenge to get her to respect my abilities and me more.

Reflections

1. In what areas of your life do you need to "reality check" yourself?

2. What stories are no longer serving you?

3. How can you change them?

Secret #27: Find a Champion

A little boy was having difficulty lifting a heavy stone. His father came along just then. Noting the boy's failure, he asked, "Are you using all of your strength?" "Yes, I am," the little boy said impatiently. "No, you are not," the father answered. "I am right here just waiting, and you haven't asked for help."

—Anonymous

This is another huge one for superachievers. I think most of us are used to taking on the world by ourselves and are afraid or too proud to ask for help. Whatever the reason we have for not asking for help, there is going to be some point in our lives when we can get to where we want to go much faster by reaching out for and accepting help.

To get where you want to go, you will need to find a champion. Champions are people who have walked the path before you, those who are where you want to be. They can certainly also serve as mentors, but their true purposes are to help pull you up to where they are (or at least closer to them than you would be if you were going it alone). A champion's role is to introduce you to his or her network and to be the recognized name endorsing you.

When I decided that I wanted a management position within the FBI, I started looking around for a champion. I found one, set up an appointment to meet with her through her assistant, and marched into her office asking her to be my mentor (I didn't think it would sound right if I asked her to be my champion). She was a very powerful woman in the organization, with ties all the way up to the head of the agency. People (nonsuperachievers) thought I was crazy for going directly to her (she was about five levels up the chain of command). Not only did I learn a lot from her, but I also became a senior manager in the organization within one year of that fateful day.

Reflections

1. Even if you weren't aware of it, as a superachiever, you've probably had a champion in your life already. Reflect on your past experiences, and identify who has helped you.

2. Who is where you currently want to be—someone that could serve as a champion for you?

3. How will you approach this champion to help you springboard to the next level?

Secret #28: Help Others

Help others achieve their dreams and you will achieve yours.
—Les Brown

As a superachiever, you are here to make a positive impact on the world, and that is done by helping others. This world needs as many positive vibes as possible, and those are created through the spreading of goodwill.

Smile at people, look them in the eyes as you pass them, and say good morning or afternoon. As you are listening to others speak about their work, hobbies, dreams, and so on, think of others you can connect them to and make introductions. Pay the toll of the person behind you. You get the idea.

On your superachiever journey, you have had the help of others—role models, champions, and teachers—so this is how you repay their kindness in helping you get to where you are. My business partner and I find great pleasure in volunteering our time speaking to youth groups, particularly girls' leadership programs for disadvantaged young ladies. Our goal is to help them realize that the entire world is open to them for whatever they want to accomplish.

Superachievers help others help themselves. Make sure you take time out from your superachieving efforts to help others, give back, and *pay it forward*.

Reflections

1. How are you helping others?

2. How do you pay it forward?

3. Think of three people in your life you can do something for—it can be as small as paying for a cup of coffee for a homeless person or as big as taking your loved ones on a fun excursion—and do it!

Secret #29: Do Whatever It Takes

What I lack in talent, I compensate with my willingness to grind it out. That is the secret of my life.

—Guy Kawasaki

Superachievers are willing to do whatever is necessary to accomplish our goals (as long as it is legal and ethical, of course!). Nothing is "below" us or too inconvenient—if it is in service of the goal, we will do it.

I remember the closest college that had the degree program I wanted was an hour away. Because I was married to a marine at the time, and we didn't have a choice about where we lived, I had no qualms about driving an hour to get my education. I organized my classes to minimize my commute, and I was thankful for the opportunity.

Even though we were a low-income family, I volunteered (worked for free!) at the local police department and used student loans to pay for childcare, because I was getting invaluable work experience before I graduated. It turns out I was able to land an $80,000-a-year job right out of college (in the 1990s), because I was willing to do whatever it took.

If you're not willing to do whatever is necessary to accomplish your goal, I recommend you look closely at it to see if it is really what you want to do. As a superachiever, if you really, really want something, you will find a way to achieve it.

Reflections

1. How willing are you to do whatever is necessary to accomplish your goals?

2. How has this level of willingness opened doors for you?

3. Reflect on a time that you overcame an obstacle to achieve a goal. What did you do, and how did it make you feel?

Secret #30: Nurture Mind, Body, and Soul

The body heals with play, the mind heals with laughter, and the spirit heals with joy.

—Proverb

This secret is all about balance. To be a superachiever in all your awesomeness, you need to be whole. "To be whole" means to be balanced in how you nurture your mind, body, and soul.

Please don't confuse this with work/life balance, as it is not the same thing. Many superachievers know what we want and go after it, so we may work a lot more than others because we love to do it. Hell, work as much as you want, as long as you nurture your mind, body, and soul.

Nurture your mind by continually improving it—not just with knowledge but also with wisdom. Do what you need to ensure the mind is your servant, not your master. Calm any busy or worrying thoughts (Secret #16), and make sure that your mind is at its healthiest to accomplish whatever you set out to achieve.

Nurture your body by eating well and exercising. Yes, a simple concept, but not always so easy. Many of us superachievers spend a lot of time in our heads and neglect our bodies. Your body is what makes your superachieving possible. Without it, there is no superachieving, because there is no you.

Nurture your soul. Whatever your beliefs are, there is a part of you that needs love, needs to be loved, needs to trust that everything will be OK, and needs to see the beauty in everything. Take the time to stop and smell the roses, to look at the beautiful sunset, to meet a friend for coffee (or wine), and to connect with your loved ones, in order to keep this part of yourself in balance.

Reflections

1. How can you nurture you mind better?

2. How can you nurture your body better?

3. How can you nurture your soul better?

Secret #31: Study Your Greats

If you want to be successful, find someone who has achieved the results you want and copy what they do and you'll achieve the same results.

—Tony Robbins

What better way to pull yourself up quicker into your dreams than to study those that have gone before you? Superachievers identify those individuals who have accomplished similar feats that we hope to achieve and study them. We read their books, consume their websites, watch interviews, and explore any other media available.

I've been known to spot a "great" at a conference, walk right up to him or her, and ask if I could have a moment of his or her time. I actually got myself invited to dinner with a group of folks and Jack Zenger, author of several books on coaching and leadership. I've been studying Steve Siebold, a million-dollar speaker, and plan on going to his workshop as soon as I make some time.

Your greats will change over time, as you get closer to what you want to achieve and when you're off to the next accomplishment. Get creative in how you learn about them, and do your best to reach out and connect with them. Almost anyone is accessible electronically these days. That is how Steve Siebold got to where he is today—interviewing thousands of people he considered world-class successes to learn how they think. A true superachiever, he didn't keep all this knowledge to himself; he then turned his newly found wisdom into a few books from which the rest of us can learn.

Reflections

1. Who are your greats?

2. What are you doing to learn from them?

3. What more could you do to learn from them?

Secret #32: Live in the Present

If you are depressed, you are living in the past. If you are anxious, you are living in the future. If you are at peace you are living in the present.

—Lao Tzu

Sometimes superachievers are so focused on the future that we forget to live in the present. When we do this, not only do we miss out on reveling in our current success, but this can also lead to frustration when we perceive that we are not moving fast enough toward our goals or dreams.

I remember when my business partner and I earned our first check and were on our way to deposit it in the bank. My mind was so far forward in the future that rather than revel in the success of earning our very first client, I was laughing at how piddly the amount was compared to what I knew we would soon be making.

It is very important to strategically plan where you want to go and what you want to accomplish, so you can ensure you attract the right people, places, and circumstances to get you there. It is equally important to focus on the present moment, to be completely immersed in the state of flow that comes with being superproductive.

Meditation can help retrain your brain to spend a little more time in the present moment. However, I wouldn't recommend going all superachiever when attempting mediation by trying to accomplish the best technique in the shortest amount of time. Meditation is simply either sitting or walking while not thinking. Of course, thoughts will occur, but your main focus during that given amount of time is to *simply be*.

Reflections

1. How often are you in the future?

2. What are some ways you can practice being in the present moment?

3. How can you tap into being in "flow" more often?

Secret #33: Celebrate Wins AND Failures

Celebrate your successes. Find some humor in your failures.
—Sam Walton

Most people pass through their accomplishments too quickly, moving on to the next one without taking the time to reflect on both the process and thinking that got them to the end goal.

Too often as superachievers, we forge quickly ahead and don't bother to look back after each win to see what we did right. By celebrating each success, we are taking the time to relish our accomplishments and learn how to replicate them.

As far as our failures go, as superachievers, we generally will examine them as learning points, but we certainly don't stop to celebrate them. Why is it important to celebrate our failures? *We took the risk to do something great.* If we don't celebrate ourselves for that, we might shy away from taking risks. Not taking risks will slow down our superachiever progress.

In celebrating your successes and your failures, you acknowledge your development—simply that you've become who you needed to be to accomplish the goal you set for yourself.

Reflections

1. How did you celebrate and learn from your last win?

2. How did you celebrate your last failure?

3. What can you do to increase your celebrations?

Secret #34: Be Positive, Not Delusional

A dream doesn't become reality through magic; it takes sweat, determination, and hard work.

—Colin Powell

To maintain maximum energy for your superachieving, it is important to remain positive, regardless of what you come up against. Positive thinking creates energy, while negative thinking consumes energy. If you think this is baloney, try the following experiment:

1. Choose a day of the week you don't have anything immensely important to achieve. Spend the first half hour of the day thinking about all of the "crap" that's going on in your life and how difficult it is going to be to face it. At the end of the day, reflect on how you felt throughout the day and your energy levels.

2. The next day, spend the first half hour thinking about how grateful you are for everything in your life and how excited you are to have been given another day on this earth to impact the world. Then, again, reflect at the end of the day on how you felt and your energy levels. Make note of the vast difference between the two days (I guarantee the difference will be huge!).

Positive thinking is a must for moving forward more quickly (and much more happily) in your life. This doesn't mean that no matter what, you must smile and laugh (this would be the delusional part—using positivity as an avoidance mechanism). There are times when you feel beat down after coming up against some tough obstacles, and you need some time to recover. It doesn't mean that you don't stand up for yourself when someone tries to take advantage of you. Rather, positive thinking means you trust that you'll get through whatever you're facing at the time.

Reflections

1. How can you create more energy for yourself through positive thinking?

2. What do you do to allow yourself to process and move through the tough times?

3. How can you ensure you're using positive thinking in an effective manner and not as an avoidance mechanism?

Secret #35: Wishing Won't Make It So

Strivers achieve what dreamers believe.

—Usher

Where most people engage in some sort of visualization (or daydreaming), superachievers visualize our goals and then jump into action. Where most people believe they've done all they could, shrug their shoulders, and leave it up to fate, superachievers, if we really want it, find ways to obtain our goals.

I'll never forget when I took my first professional position after graduating from college. I took over a crime analysis unit at a local police department. In those days, the department was quite progressive to even have this type of unit, so there wasn't a big budget. Because I wanted to take the unit to the next level, I came up with a list of about $60,000 in equipment, software programs, and training needed to have a state-of-the-art unit—a huge budget at that time. Being a superachiever, I didn't let a little pesky thing like a limited budget get in the way. I made it my mission to find and apply for as many grants as possible.

Not too long after applying for my first grant, I found that we were awarded a grant large enough to get everything on my wish list as well as additional surveillance equipment for our investigations and narcotics units.

As discussed in Secret #18, it is important to set an intention and get a crystal clear vision. Here's where superachievers leave others in the dust—once we have visions set, we jump into action, and nothing can stop us from achieving our goals.

Reflections

1. What do you visualize/daydream about?

2. What steps have you taken to make your visualizations/daydreams real?

3. What more could you do?

Secret #36: Even in the Darkest Moments...Have Faith

If fear is cultivated, it will become stronger. If faith is cultivated, it will achieve mastery.

—John Paul Jones

When you go back and look at the darkest moments in your life, do you see how they have helped shape you into the superachiever you are today? While in the midst of those darkest moments, superachievers have faith that "this too shall pass" and they will be better people for it. Like Secret #2, superachievers know that adversity really is a gift.

The key to this secret is that, no matter what, superachievers have the confidence and faith that we will get through it and even thrive because of it. No matter what has happened in my life—losing my father to a five-year battle with cancer, going through a divorce with two small children, dealing with a boss that was a terror, and helping my son through an ordeal with his biological father—I knew I would make it through and be a better person for it.

Having faith leads to being superconscious of your thoughts and actions while going through the dark moments. This is another bonus, because, as a superachiever, you learn from them and consider them a developmental opportunity.

Reflections

1. What have been the darkest moments of your life?

2. What kind of faith did you have in yourself during those moments?

3. How can you improve upon the faith and confidence you have in yourself?

Secret #37: Desperation Smells Bad

Desperation is like stealing from the mafia; you stand a good chance of attracting the wrong attention.

—Douglas Horton

Desperation is "a state of despair, typically one that results in rash or extreme behavior." Superachievers, regardless of our circumstances, do not come across as desperate to others. We are cool, calm, and collected.

As stated in Secret #36, superachievers know that no matter how dire our circumstances, we will get through, so there is no need to act in a desperate manner. People have a pretty good radar for smelling desperation and when confronted with it will either feel sympathy for the other person or a need to get away from him or her (as if it is contagious).

When I first joined the world of small-business owners, I went to a lot of networking events. I once watched a coach pressure a woman into a sample session within five minutes of meeting her. Maybe he was just an aggressive guy, but he smelled of desperation. She finally agreed because she felt bad for him and then later canceled the session.

Desperation is a state of mind. Even if, as a superachiever, we were penniless and in our darkest moment, we would still have hope and the certainty that we would soon be able to change our circumstances. Superachievers do not resort to extreme and aggressive behavior. Rather, we assertively go after our goals, *knowing* that in the end, we will be successful.

Reflections

1. What are your thoughts about desperation being a state of mind?

2. How can you be more assertive versus aggressive in achieving your goals?

3. What do you do when you are in seemingly desperate circumstances?

Secret #38: It Is What It Is

No matter how bad something gets, no matter where you come from, you can achieve anything. I really do believe that.

—Hill Harper

Sometimes, as superachievers, we get frustrated when we're not moving toward goals as fast as we think we should be. We can be quite successful at complaining about it, especially when there are obstacles in our way that are seemingly insurmountable. When we find ourselves in these situations, we need to remind ourselves that *it is what it is* and to get over it.

Sure, sometimes I'll give myself twenty minutes or so to have a pity party, but then, that's it—it is time to let it go or do something about it. I learned this lesson on a large scale several years ago when I was in a highly specialized position (the only position like it in the federal government), and I got *the boss from hell.* I knew he would be my boss for at least two to three years. My poor family had to hear about every unbelievable thing he did for the almost two years I worked for him.

Initially, I spent a lot of my time complaining and feeling stuck. Then I decided to quit [bleeping] around, put on my big-girl pants, and do something about it—because I did have a choice. I was choosing to stay in that situation even though I was extremely unhappy. I didn't need to choose to stay stuck any longer, even if it meant switching career fields.

I went back to school part time for an advanced degree in education and started networking with folks from our organization's training division. Very soon I transferred to that division and received a promotion. Now I am very grateful for that horrible boss, because I wouldn't be where I am today if it weren't for him.

Reflections

1. What do you find yourself complaining about most often?

2. How can you either do something about it or let it go?

3. There is always a choice involved—what is your choice in the situation?

Secret #39: To Thine Own Self Be True

Just be yourself. Be honest, work toward a goal, and you'll achieve it.

—Emraan Hashini

I like to think of superachievers as chameleons—we are able to easily change our behavior and how we speak around others to make them feel more comfortable. This is a great skill to have in connecting with others, because rapport building is key to getting ahead in life. As a matter of fact, this falls under Robert Cialdini's six principles of influence—the principle of likeability, which states that people like and are therefore influenced by those who are similar to them.

Being a chameleon with others is a great skill to have—to a point. There is a fine line that can be crossed where, as superachievers, we can find ourselves working harder to make others comfortable around us, rather than being ourselves. One of the byproducts of this issue is Secret #12, the outshine syndrome. Ultimately, you begin tucking away too many parts of yourself when connecting with others.

The solution is to be aware when this is happening. Awareness is the first step (in pretty much everything) and can also be the hardest. Being aware of when I am in a detrimental *chameleon mode* with an individual has been a lifelong struggle. Once you become aware of your ability to morph with others, you'll be able to figure out exactly where that fine line exists. A technique I've started recently using is to set an alarm for an evening reflection. It only needs to last for a few minutes. To start off the reflection, I ask myself, "Were you true to yourself today?"

Reflections

1. Examine several past interactions with others. How were you able to be a chameleon to help the other person feel more comfortable?

2. At what point in those interactions did you stop being who you are to help them with their comfort level?

3. Were you true to yourself today?

Secret #40: Choose Your Stories Carefully

As a rule, we find what we look for. We achieve what we get ready for.

—James Cash Penney

In Secret #26, I introduced Argyris's Ladder of Inference in how we develop our beliefs. These beliefs are really our stories, and we have them for everything. Superachievers are intuitively aware of this and do our darndest to choose only empowering stories.

Even though we are superachievers, we are also human, and sometimes we forget we have the power to choose our own reality. Being cognitively aware of this (not just intuitively), we are able to choose our stories in the moment. For example, I was recently in a situation where I decided the person I was speaking with was being difficult for the sake of being difficult. I realized in that moment that I was creating a story that wasn't in my best interest, because I was getting extremely frustrated. Rather, I decided that my new story would be that the individual was nervous and experiencing a lack of self-confidence. Regardless of why the person was being seemingly difficult, by changing my story, I was less frustrated and more compassionate.

Once you become more cognitively aware of this process, it is easier to change stories in the moment. What is more difficult is identifying and changing the stories we've had for a very long time. I am still overcoming the story I developed in childhood that my high energy is annoying to others. I am working on replacing it with a new story: "I am a superachiever and the world needs me to show up fully." (This book is a huge step in owning that new story.)

Reflections

1. What types of stories are you creating about you and your life?

2. How can you become more cognitively aware of when you are creating a story in the moment?

3. What old stories do you need to let go of?

Secret #41: Be Selective of the Company You Keep

Successful people will always tell you you can do something. It's the people who have never accomplished anything who will always discourage you from trying to achieve excellent things.
—Lou Holtz

You can do all kinds of internal work, and you can be amazing at forgiving others and letting go; however, there will still be some people in your life who choose to continue to live in their own dysfunction. As a superachiever who wants to change the world for the better, it is hard to "let" these people wallow in their dysfunction when you can see how much happier they would be if they would quit repeating their actions.

This is a hard lesson to learn—you don't "let" anyone do anything. We each have complete control over our path in life but not the paths of others. When these people choose to have dysfunction in their lives, and it holds you back by having them in your life, it would serve you to eliminate them from your life (or at least greatly reduce your exposure).

I once had a friend who was addicted to drama. Although we loved each other dearly, I often found myself caught up in the middle of her drama. It was a heart-wrenching decision, but I eventually decided I was better off without her in my life. After the initial grieving period, I felt a tremendous weight lift, and I was free to get back to superachieving.

Reflections

1. How do you try to "save" others from their dysfunction?

2. Who is in your life right now that is currently holding you back as a superachiever?

3. What are you going to do about it?

Secret #42: Remember Unconditional Love?

The ultimate lesson all of us have to learn is unconditional love, which includes not only others, but ourselves as well.
—Elizabeth Kubler-Ross

Superachievers, by our very nature, set the bar extremely high for ourselves. We have very high expectations of ourselves and are continually striving to get better, better, and even better. This inner drive is what essentially makes us superachievers. While this is the foundation of our superpowers, it can also lead us to being very hard on ourselves.

People, in general, are hard on themselves. It is in our nature as human beings, and superachievers excel in this area. One way to keep from beating yourself up too much is to remind yourself of unconditional love in some way. Unconditional love is simply loving oneself or others without any conditions such as "I love and feel good about myself regardless of whether or not I'm achieving my goals." (For some of us superachievers, love is tied into our achievements, something we learned in childhood.)

When I think of unconditional love, I think of beloved pets—specifically, my cat Samantha. She greets me as soon as I wake up in the morning, follows me around, is always ready for a cuddle, and will often stare at me with what I call "soft eyes" (in a loving way). When I find myself being especially unforgiving of my performance in a particular area, I'll take a time out to cuddle with her, or look at a photo of her to remind myself to see *me* through her eyes—with love and total adoration.

You may not be a pet person, but find something in your life that reminds you of unconditional love, and use it as a reminder to treat yourself with love and compassion as you are on your superachiever journey.

Reflections

1. What kind of expectations do you hold for yourself?

2. What do you do when you don't meet those expectations?

3. What can serve as a reminder to have compassion and love for yourself?

Secret #43: Unable to Spend Time Alone? Ruh-Roh!

Solitude is creativity's best friend, and solitude is refreshment for our souls.

—Naomi Judd

No matter how much of an extrovert you are (i.e., someone who gets his or her energy by being with others), as a superachiever, you need to be comfortable with solitude. If you are one of those folks who doesn't like to be alone, so much so that you have the TV or radio on for background noise, there is some work to be done. As Scooby Doo would say, "Ruh-roh!"

Solitude means simply "to be alone." Superachievers are major go-getters, always in action; therefore, it is important we take some time in solitude to refresh our mind, body, and soul. By spending time alone, the superachiever brain gets a much needed break, increasing focus and concentration. Solitude provides the space necessary to work through solutions to challenges, to come up with new and creative ideas, and to recharge the brain and body for superproductivity.

Solitude doesn't mean that you have to sit quietly and meditate for hours on end or go into the woods by yourself. These are certainly options; however, they are not requirements. You can even consider the time you spend in the shower (as long as you are alone) as a form of solitude.

The shower is where I get a lot of my ideas because I am relaxed and focused on getting clean, allowing my brain and body to get a bit of a break from rushing around to the next goal to be accomplished.

There is not a specific amount of recommended solitude per day; rather, it is unique to each individual. You must listen to your body and mind to determine the right amount for you. You get the point—let's not put a bunch of rules around solitude. Just make sure to spend some downtime alone to maximize your superachieving awesomeness.

Reflections

1. How comfortable are you with solitude?

2. Examine the last few weeks of your life. How much was spent in solitude versus being in action and with others?

3. How can you spend more time in solitude?

Secret #44: Worrying Is a Waste of Mental Energy

Difficult times have helped me to understand better than before how infinitely rich and beautiful life is in every way and that so many things that one goes worrying about are of no importance whatsoever.

—Isak Dinesen

Superachievers need a lot of energy to do the amazing things of which we are capable. Therefore, it is paramount we don't allow any of that precious energy to be wasted. Worrying wastes a lot of energy. As stated in Secret #34, negative thinking consumes energy, and worrying is definitely a form of negative thinking.

Worrying leads to stress, and stress can lead to physical illness. Stress is essentially the unexperienced experience. When you spend your precious time and energy worrying about what *could* happen, you are taking time and energy away from achieving your goals, and ultimately, your dreams.

What do you do when you find yourself in a worry spiral (when you go down the "rabbit hole" of worrying)? This is when you activate several of the secrets in this book. Find yourself some solitude (Secret #43); identify which of the saboteurs is feeding your negative thoughts, and tell it to go on vacation (Secret #16); and then start looking at your problem as a challenge to overcome, funneling all that energy to do something good (Secret #24).

Reflections

1. How often do you find yourself worrying?

2. What are the typical things you worry about?

3. How will you get yourself out of the worry loop the next time it happens?

Secret #45: Just Do It Already!

To achieve great things, two things are needed: a plan, and not quite enough time.

—Leonard Bernstein

Superachievers don't often fall victim to procrastination, but sometimes it does happen. When this rare occurrence rears its ugly head, it can be very frustrating for us, because we are used to moving at lightning speed through our to-do list.

There are many reasons humans procrastinate. Luckily, there are two simple questions superachievers can ask ourselves to break through the procrastination barrier. The first question to ask is, "Do I really want this?" For example, I've wanted to write a book for years. Every time I came up with an idea and outlined it, I sat on it for a long period of time. It's not that I didn't want to write a book; after I asked myself if I really wanted it, I realized that I didn't want to write *that* book.

After we've answered the first question in the affirmative, the next question to ask is, "How can I motivate myself to *just do it already?*" Once I settled on a particular topic that I truly wanted to write about (superachieving!), I examined what would best motivate me to get it written. I decided nothing would be more motivating than to start booking speaking engagements. So I booked my first speaking engagement five months out and got to writing.

Reflections

1. What pattern do you find in how you procrastinate?

2. What are you procrastinating on right now?

3. Is it something you really want? If so, how can you motivate yourself to just do it already?

Secret #46: There Will Be Sacrifices

You have to put in many, many, many tiny efforts that nobody sees or appreciates before you can achieve anything worthwhile.
—Brian Tracy

Anyone who tells you that all you need to do is set an intention and wait for the planets to align for your dreams to come to fruition is full of the stuff that a bull leaves lying around on a pasture. Setting your intentions is important, but superachievers know that achievement is earned through hard work and sacrifice. To others, hard work and sacrifice can seem to be both negative and daunting. To superachievers, they are a means of accomplishing a dream, and therefore, a part of the journey—neither good nor bad.

For superachieving purposes, sacrifice means to give up something in order to gain what you desire. One example is giving up a full night's sleep for a few months to work on a major project or choosing to commute a full hour (or two) for the program you desire, rather than going to a local school. Sacrifice is part of the equation for superachievers, so we don't give it a second thought; we do what needs to be done.

I can't even fathom the number of times I've had to sacrifice in some way to achieve my dreams. One of my largest sacrifices was to walk away from a secure, six-figure job in order to achieve my dream of owning my own business. I knew that I would need to start to budget again and only buy what I absolutely needed (versus wanted). I was willing to make a change in lifestyle in order both to be happy and eventually make more than I could have ever made while in government service. I've never even considered looking back—the sacrifice is worth it to be living my dream.

Reflections

1. What are your thoughts on sacrificing for achievement?

2. What have you sacrificed in the past to achieve your goals?

3. What are you sacrificing right now to achieve your goals?

Secret #47: There's Always a Way!

Nothing stops a man who desires to achieve. Every obstacle is simply a course to develop his achievement muscle. It is a strengthening of his powers of accomplishment.

—Thomas Carlyle

One thing I've learned on my superachiever journey is that there is *always* a way to achieve a goal—if I really want it. Some may believe superachievers can be unrealistic in this area. I've actually been called irrational, but it was quickly retracted when I demonstrated to the person that the seemingly impossible goal was achieved.

When superachievers come upon obstacles to our goals, we will find a way around them, often by using nontraditional approaches. Most people keep trying different actions to get *through* the obstacle, but the superachiever will take it a step further and look at a way *around* it. We will step back and examine what assumptions we are making about the obstacles, we will look at how our thinking affects the results we are getting, and we will consult with others who think differently in order to get another perspective (Secret #17).

I'll never forget when one of my colleagues referred to me as the little red sports car that doesn't care if a train gets in her way, because she just drives around it. I thought it was an interesting metaphor (not something one normally would think about) and also very true. Superachievers are able to come up with unorthodox ways of getting what we want. No budget? Get a grant. Not enough money coming in? Pick up some odd jobs. Lack of resources? Call in your network. You get the idea.

Reflections

1. What are your thoughts on obstacles?

2. How have you overcome obstacles in the past?

3. What is the most unique, creative way that you have overcome an obstacle in the past?

Secret #48: Shit Happens

We may achieve climate, but weather is thrust upon us.

—O. Henry

No matter how well you plan, shit happens. The superachiever understands when this happens that it is not the end of the world. The superachiever always has one or more contingency plans, because we expect shit to happen. While everyone else is running around frantic like Chicken Little, the superachiever is cool, calm, and collected while implementing plan B, C, or D. Because we have conditioned ourselves in this manner, we are better able to deal when the unexpected happens.

A few years ago, I was driving with my family through a shopping center and noticed that a man had passed out in his car (which was still running) while waiting in the turn lane. I also noticed people pacing nervously around his car while on the phone, presumably calling emergency services. I calmly stopped my car, put the hazards on, asked my family to stay in the car, and walked up to his car. I looked at his chest and saw that he was still breathing, and then I reached in and took the keys out of the ignition. There were about five frantic people around, and no one thought to turn off his car. Imagine if his foot had slipped off the break. (If you're curious, it turns out he was drunk and had passed out.)

The point is that when you expect the proverbial shit to hit the fan and are ready to deal with it, you can keep your wits about you and calmly face the issue at hand. Superachievers excel at this because we have practiced it for years while going after our goals. In essence, superachievers are OK with not being OK all the time, which allows us to continue moving forward in every aspect of our lives.

Reflections

1. What are your thoughts on "Shit happens; it's not the end of the world"?

2. How do you prepare for the unexpected?

3. When was a time you were able to respond to a situation being the only one that was cool, calm, and collected?

Secret #49: When the Going Gets Tough...Take a Nap

It's how you deal with failure that determines how you achieve success.

—Charlotte Whitton

Typical superachievers are so full of gusto to accomplish our goals that when we face a setback, we tend to dig our heels in and either push harder to move forward or find another way around the obstacle. This is a great response for superachieving; however, it shouldn't be the only response. Sometimes, we need to step away from a goal momentarily.

I learned from my husband (who jokingly is going to write the counter series to *Quit [Bleeping] Around,* titled *Keep [Bleeping] Around*) that sometimes one just needs to take a nap. In order to move forward, especially when dealing with a complicated obstacle to a particular goal, you need to slow down or back off for a little while. By taking a break from achieving your goal, you are giving your mind and body a break from the *go, go, go* mode that superachievers tend to fall into.

Not too long ago, I was getting frustrated because I had set a goal to develop an online suite of courses for my professional development firm. It seemed like every time I tried to move forward with finding a platform for the courses, an obstacle would present itself, mainly in overpriced platforms that had too many bells and whistles for what we wanted. When I would find an online-course platform that was within our budget, it didn't have the precise tools for our needs. After pushing and pushing to locate the perfect platform, I decided to drop the project for two weeks and focus on something else. About a week later, I received an email about a new platform that would easily integrate with our current website and was quite cost effective. By letting go and not pushing, I was able to remain open to other options that came my way.

Reflections

1. What do you do when the "going gets tough"?

2. When have you backed off of a goal in the past?

3. How did taking a break help you?

Secret #50: Work Smarter AND Harder

You've got brains in your head, you've got feet in your shoes. You can steer yourself any direction you choose.

—Dr. Suess

Superachievers love to work hard. Accused of being workaholics by some, we don't see working hard (and long hours) as a bad thing. When you love the process of achieving goals, you give yourself to it completely. Not only do we work harder, we also work smarter—for superachievers, the two go hand in hand. We don't simply work smarter to not work harder; we do both. This is why superachievers are superproductive. We get creative in how we do our work and create systems for maximum efficiency and effectiveness.

One question I constantly ask myself is "How can I make this process better?" As I improve the process, I get my work done more quickly, allowing me to move onto the next goal faster. When I was with the government, I came up with a checklist system for producing analytical reports and had refined the system enough to where I was producing up to thirty reports a month. (The unit goal was two reports per analyst per month.) When charged with creating online college courses for my position as an online adjunct professor, I developed a system that allowed me to produce a full-semester college course in as little as eight hours.

Superachievers are always looking for more efficient and effective processes for being productive. We will research processes, ask others to demonstrate the processes they utilize, go to classes, and so on, all in hopes of finding ways to work both smarter and harder.

Reflections

1. What ways have you identified that help you work smarter?

2. What are your thoughts on hard work?

3. How can you improve your current processes to allow you to work both smarter and harder?

Secret #51: Suck It Up!
(a.k.a. Mental Toughness)

Refuse to emotionally succumb to the negative events around you and tap into your mental toughness to thrive in any environment.
—Steve Siebold

I think of mental toughness as grit—digging your heels in and doing what needs to be done, knowing that you will get through whatever it is and emerge on top. It is persevering when life gets tough while still believing that you have what it takes to achieve. Superachievers are mentally tough. Although some may be predisposed biologically to be mentally tough, I believe it is a decision that we make. It is a perspective or frame of reference that the superachiever adopts in order to be a superachiever.

I've never had to practice mental toughness more than when I was an athlete in training. Superachiever athletes definitely have an edge in the mental toughness department. When I was a teenager, I would compete in junior-level tennis tournaments (under eighteen) up to the national level. This required a minimum of two hours of practice and drilling on the courts every day—rain, snow, or shine—as well as time in the gym for conditioning both cardio and strength. Blisters, sore muscles, and upset tummies would not deter the daily practice that would move me toward my goal. And once I was on the court in a competitive match, nothing else existed but the ball, my opponent, and myself.

Superachievers have a certain grit that allows us to stay focused on the goal and achieve it regardless of what comes our way. How we achieve mental toughness is through choice and lots of practice.

Reflections

1. Do you have mental toughness?

2. Describe a time in your life when mental toughness was the key factor in getting you through the circumstances you were in.

3. What are some ways you can improve your mental toughness?

Secret #52: My Body Is My Temple

Man, like other organisms, is so perfectly coordinated that he may easily forget, whether awake or asleep, that he is a colony of cells in action, and that it is the cells which achieve, through him, what he has the illusion of accomplishing himself.

—Albert Claude

We generally don't realize how important our bodies are until we get sick. Superachievers are like the Energizer bunny—we keep going and going until we can't anymore. It takes a strong cold or flu to sideline us, and then we are miserable for several days until our energy bounces back. We tend to be horrible sick folks—our loved ones are just as miserable as we are when we we're out of commission because of all of our complaining (unless we are so sick all we can do is sleep).

As I sit here and write this chapter, I am recovering from mistreating my body. I got on a superachiever high by being superproductive and forgetting to stop and rest, eat properly, and give my body some good old tender loving care (TLC), and I am paying for it. As I sit on the couch, my body protesting that I am not totally reclined and doing nothing, I am kicking myself for allowing it to happen again. As superachievers, we can get so focused on our goals that we forget to take care of our bodies. Our bodies will take a pretty good beating; however, there comes a point where they say "enough" and force us to take a break.

In order to fully own our superachieverhood, we must, must, must take care of ourselves. This means proper hydration, rest, nutrition, and exercise. Our bodies give us the energy to do what we need to do—the energy to keep our minds running at full steam ahead. Without our bodies, we are literally nothing.

Taking care of our bodies is quite simple but not necessarily easy. We must make the time to plan out proper nutrition (including going shopping and preparing the food). We must plan out our exercise and schedule it in our calendars. There are a lot of apps for our various devices that appeal to the superachiever nature, allowing us to set daily eating, hydration, and exercise goals as well as to track our sleep to ensure we are getting enough. Taking care of our bodies should be a priority, not an afterthought.

Reflections

1. How often does your body have to remind you to take care of it?

2. How do you ensure you get proper rest, hydration, nutrition, and exercise?

3. How can you do even better at taking care of yourself?

Secret #53: Blaming Others Is for Losers

Accept responsibility for your life. Know that it is you who will get you where you want to go, no one else.

—Les Brown

One of the main ingredients of a superachiever is how we take responsibility for ourselves, our choices, our circumstances, and, ultimately, our lives. We know that who we are and the current circumstances we are in are due to the choices we have made and that if we are not happy with our current lots in life, it is our responsibility to change them. We do not blame others for our circumstances nor do we expect others to rescue us.

When superachievers find ourselves in circumstances we are not happy with, having trouble moving forward with a particular goal, we will engage in systems thinking to track down how our choices got us to this point (more on this in Secret #69). We then take action to get ourselves out of those circumstances rather than waiting for someone else to save the day.

I remember when I first started my professional development firm, I was getting frustrated because the development of new clients was taking longer than I expected (as a superachiever, I had very high expectations.) I wanted to start earning a paycheck from the business quickly. My frustration was an indicator to me that I needed to step back and examine my current circumstances (Secret #47), my expectations, and how my choices resulted in this situation. After working through it, I realized that I was putting too much pressure on obtaining a financial flow from one specific area. To alleviate my frustration, I simply took on three more coaching clients. This freed me up to focus on bringing in more business for the company, and we ended up getting five small government contracts over about eight weeks.

Reflections

1. How often do you find yourself blaming others for your circumstances?

2. What are key indicators that you need to examine how you got yourself into your current circumstances (i.e., frustration, anger, etc.)?

3. Describe a recent time that you found yourself in circumstances you were not happy with and how you were able to change them.

Secret #54: Don't Have Enough Time? Bullshit!

Time is what we want most, but what we use worst.

—William Penn

Hearing people say that they "don't have enough time" is a pet peeve for superachievers. A superachiever knows that we make time for what is important to us, and we maximize our use of time so we can be more productive with it, accomplishing whatever we have chosen to achieve.

In modern society, it has become a badge of importance (or martyrdom) to talk about how busy one is and how there isn't enough time in the day to accomplish all of one's responsibilities. When I hear this, I see it as a lack in ability to prioritize one's time and maximize the efficiency and effectiveness in which it is used.

By carefully prioritizing responsibilities and working both smarter *and* harder (Secret #50), a superachiever is able to accomplish much more than the average person. I have always worked at least two jobs while raising my kids, even fitting in a couple of college degrees along the way. Many people couldn't understand how this could possibly be done, assuming that I wasn't spending quality time with my children. I had lots of quality time with my kids, all while enjoying myself immensely, as I was highly productive in my full time job as well as my part time positions as an adjunct professor at multiple online colleges. All of this was accomplished by carefully scheduling out my time and deciding what I needed to personally do, what I needed to delegate to others, and what I needed to dump, meaning I didn't need to have it on my to-do list. Superachievers understand that we don't have to do all of the tasks ourselves, and many of them don't really need to be done at all.

Reflections

1. What responsibilities and/or tasks do you currently do that are a priority in achieving your goals?

2. What responsibilities and/or tasks do you currently do that you could have others do?

3. What responsibilities and/or tasks do you currently do that you could stop doing—tasks that are not in furtherance of your goals?

Secret #55: Connection with Others Is Nonnegotiable

No man or woman is an island. To exist just for yourself is meaningless. You can achieve the most satisfaction when you feel related to some greater purpose in life, something greater than yourself.

—Dennis Waitley

Superachieving can be very lonely if we don't allow ourselves to connect with others. Because of our concern with how others will receive us (jealousy, annoyance, appreciation) and the tendency to move quickly ahead of others in both thinking and tasks, superachievers can be reticent when it comes to personal connections. Regardless of this vulnerability, it is important for superachievers to connect with others. Our connections are what make us better human beings and allow us to accomplish more.

When I started my professional development firm, I was used to working on my own and I didn't want to be slowed down in any way, so I didn't even consider involving others. Once I got the business up and running, I quickly realized that I would need additional help to take the business where I wanted it to go. After much deliberation, I called in a dear friend of many years whom I trusted and I knew accepted me for who I am. Since she became by business partner, we've been able to accomplish so much more together than I could have on my own, and our connection is that much deeper...all because I decided to be vulnerable and ask for help rather than remain the "lone superachiever."

Reflections

1. How well do you connect with others?

2. What has stopped you in the past from connecting with others?

3. How can you connect with others more?

Secret #56: Beware of Energy Vampires

Avoid cynical and negative people like the plague. They are killers of potential.

—Rick Pitino

We all have them in our lives—people that seem to suck the life out of us after we've spent some time with them. They could be family members, friends, or work colleagues. They often leave us feeling tired, cranky, and emotionally empty after sometimes only a few minutes in our presence.

Superachievers are keenly aware of energy vampires, and we either severely limit our exposure to them or completely remove them from our lives. We know that allowing these individuals to persist in being present in our lives will wear us down emotionally, even physically, *and* that is unacceptable for all the great things a superachiever needs to accomplish in order to make this world a better place. This doesn't mean that, as superachievers, we don't go through an internal struggle throughout this process. By our very nature, superachievers want to help those around us, but we understand that we can't help those that don't want help.

Thankfully, I learned this lesson at a young age, and I am very sensitive to how I feel after spending time with energy vampires. If there is too much negativity, I find a way to relocate myself in a respectful manner. Sometimes it's not so easy, but it needs to be done. Don't let these types of people pull you down into their grave of misery—do what you can for them and then move on. The world needs you to be at the top of your game to accomplish what you were put on this earth to do.

Reflections

1. How have you dealt with energy vampires in the past?

2. Who in your life, right now, is an energy vampire?

3. How do you plan to either limit your exposure to that person or eliminate that person from your life completely?

Secret #57: For Goodness' Sake, Get Some Coaching!

If you wish to achieve worthwhile things in your personal and career life, you must become a worthwhile person in your own self-development.

—Brian Tracy

Superachievers are all about self-development—how can I make myself even better? OK, now that I'm better, how can I make myself great? OK, now that I'm great, how can I be even more exceptional? You get the point...It is all about personal growth. Dare I even say that we can be "growth junkies"?

One thing, more than all the development programs combined, that can accelerate growth is *coaching*. I am quite dismayed when I come across individuals who ask, "Why do I need coaching? Nothing is wrong with me." I wish they would understand what superachievers do—that quality coaching is a catapult to help you grow at sometimes lightning speed. A good coach, one who asks you questions to help you dig deeper into yourself, discovering even more talents and challenging you to step further into your potential, is a necessity for going big and ultimately accomplishing your dreams. Do some research on your greats (Secret #31)—I bet that they have more than one coach to continually challenge them to be even better.

Since I first discovered coaching several years ago, I have had a coach that has helped me realize how much more I have to offer and has assisted me in quieting those negative voices in my head that were leading me to hide who I was around others to make them feel better. This book is a product of that self-discovery journey, and it is only the beginning.

Reflections

1. What are your thoughts on coaching?

2. Do you currently utilize the services of a coach?

3. If you don't, when will you start? If you do, how can you work with a coach to step further into your potential?

Secret #58: Curiosity May Have Killed the Cat, But...

When you're curious, you find lots of interesting things to do.
—Walt Disney

All of us have been kids at one point, so we are very familiar with the "why" phase of childhood. Most kids go through a stage when they get curious about the world and ask all kinds of "why" questions, totally exhausting the parent that takes the time to answer. Superachievers never grow out of this stage. We are curious about everything and want to soak up as much knowledge and wisdom as we can. Sometimes our curiosity can even get us in trouble. We subscribe to the old saying that "curiosity may have killed the cat, but satisfaction brought him back."

Superachievers, depending on what particular areas we cherish the most, can spend hours being curious about particular topics. For example, my big curiosity is about human behavior. So I spent my first fifteen years in the field of criminal justice studying humans who break societal norms. Then I moved into professional development and coaching; I am curious about how people can improve in their personal and professional lives, how they can effectively lead others, how our thought process can either help or hinder the us, and so on. I try different tactics with different people to see what works, how my actions impact others, and how I can better relate to others. It is a continual "human behavior experiment" that serves as a puzzle I must solve so that I can help others find a solution to their obstacles. Other superachievers may devote their time to being curious about the law, or the culinary arts, or engineering, or physics, or science, or the many other disciplines that can help make this world a better place.

Reflections

1. What are you curious about?

2. How has your insatiable curiosity helped you move forward with your goals?

3. What do you need to be more curious about?

Secret #59: Being Risk Averse Is like Dying a Slow Death

Only those who dare to fail greatly can ever achieve greatly.
—Robert Kennedy

In order to achieve great things, you must be willing to take a whole range of risks—from the wimpy, little risks to the big *holy shit* risks. Superachievers know that calculated risks are part of the game plan and embrace them as a way forward.

The key to taking risks is to understand fully what you are getting into—conducting a cost/benefit analysis for whether the risk is worth the advantage it provides in moving forward more quickly toward a goal. Unfortunately, there isn't a *one-size-fits-all* formula. This is an individual decision, as the same risk could be more beneficial (or costly) depending on the current circumstances of the superachiever.

Things to consider in the analysis include: If the risk pays off (i.e., works), what will be gained? If the risk doesn't pay off (i.e., doesn't work), will it at least be a valuable learning experience? Does taking the risk have a chance of moving closer to the intended goal, or will failing move one further away from the goal?

While my children were younger, I was less apt to take the *holy shit* risks that I do today, especially when I was the main breadwinner in the household. I chose the security of a government position while I worked on a number of goals, such as an advanced education, becoming an expert in my field, and so on. However, I knew I would eventually need to spread my wings and leave the security of the nest if I wanted to accomplish my biggest goals (a.k.a. dreams) of being an author, professional speaker, and running my own company. As soon as I had fewer financial responsibilities and a loving and supportive husband, I took the leap. It hasn't been an easy road into small-business ownership, writing a book, and positioning myself as a professional speaker, but it has been very rewarding. I've learned a lot, and I am free to fly as high as I please now.

Reflections

1. Reflect on your current level of risk taking. What are some of the little risks you've taken lately?

2. What are some of the *holy shit* risks you've taken?

3. How can you increase your risk tolerance to take more of the big calculated risks?

Secret #60: A Little Humor Can Go a Long Way

There are people who can achieve huge success in life, while adding a bit of fun and a splash of color to this increasingly grey world.

—Peter James

What would life be without humor? Pretty damn boring, that's for sure! Why not enjoy the journey, both the valleys and the peaks, with a little laughter? Superachievers keep motivated and upbeat by finding a little humor in almost everything, as laughter is reenergizing.

Laughter helps to relieve tension during stressful situations. It is good for the respiratory and circulatory systems, all while releasing feel-good hormones to calm the nervous system. Who wouldn't want to view the world with wonder and amusement, with all of these great benefits?

I am one of those folks who has a continuous running commentary of humorous outtakes in my head. This has sometimes gotten me in trouble as I laugh out loud by accident during a "serious" meeting. More often than not though, it has kept me sane when having to function in a world that sometimes feels like it is moving in slow motion. It is an amazing coping mechanism to help me get through the tough times as much as it is a high when things are going well.

During the time period that I had the boss from hell, humor was the only thing that helped me get through the day. By finding amusement in whatever current tactic he was attempting to use to manipulate his employees, I was able to separate myself from the situation and become an observer. As an amused observer studying the childish antics of a fortysomething-year-old man who was in way over his head, his frustrating behavior became much more tolerable.

Reflections

1. How have you used humor to help you get through the tough times?

2. How have you used humor to help you enjoy the good times?

3. How can you use humor more in your life to help you achieve even more?

Secret #61: Give Everything, Then Give Some More

The only question to ask yourself is, how much are you willing to sacrifice to achieve this success?

—Larry Flynt

Superachievers are completely dedicated and passionate about our goals and, ultimately, our dreams. We give everything we have in achieving whatever we choose to accomplish. The superachiever invests mentally, emotionally, and physically into getting what we want for ourselves and for others.

What does "giving everything you've got and then give it some more" look like? It looks like a singular focus until the goal is accomplished. When it gets tough, or even seems impossible, superachievers dig in our heels and keep going. When we face the 131st failure in our attempt to accomplish a goal, we dust ourselves off and try for the 132nd time.

I purposely decided to have children at a very young age for a number of reasons. I also decided that, no matter what, I was going to get a college degree. I had planned to have my first child between my sophomore and junior years so that I would have two years with my child before I started a full-time career. I ended up only missing one class when I gave birth to my daughter.

Then I learned that my first husband was transferred to a different part of the state. This move would significantly delay my progress in college. While waiting two months to move, I took a few child-development-related classes to better prepare myself as a parent. I also became pregnant with my second child (why not make the best use of the delay?). After we moved, I quickly applied to the nearest four-year college and found I couldn't start until the fall. I kept myself busy for nine months raising two babies, and then I began the almost daily one-hour commute to and from school. After much sacrifice and hard work, I earned my first degree six years after high school. Holy cow, was that a major celebration!

Reflections

1. Recall a time when you have given it all you had and then even a bit more. How did you feel when you finally accomplished your goal?

2. How do you fully immerse yourself in the process of achieving your goals/dreams?

3. How can you give even more of yourself to accomplishing your goals and, ultimately, your dreams?

Secret #62: Don't Settle. Ever!

The biggest human temptation is to settle for too little.
—Thomas Merton

Superachievers don't settle. Ever! If we really want something, we will go after it and never, ever, ever, settle for less than what we want. Through sheer will and determination, we will get precisely what we set our minds to—which may take more time than expected and involve more failures than expected, but we will eventually achieve it.

Some have surprise pregnancies and then give up on finishing school. Others might try and try to get that promotion and then give up because they got tired of trying. Some give up on a favorite sport because they decided that they just weren't good enough and weren't willing to put in the time and effort it requires to be better. It can happen in any area, but not for superachievers; we do not engage in this type of behavior. If we want it, we will not accept less. We do not settle. Ever!

I have set three different dreams for my life that are proving to be a bit elusive; they have taken me years to make any progress, but I am not giving up. These goals include being debt-free, getting to and maintaining my goal weight for the rest of my life, and speaking to ten thousand people in some sort of keynote address. I've had some of these dreams since I entered adulthood, and I will have to continue to work on them for several more years before I attain all of them; however, I refuse to settle for anything less.

Reflections

1. Have you ever settled for something? If so, what happened?

2. How have you had the determination to get what you want, regardless of how long it takes or how many failures you've had?

3. What are you working toward right now that you refuse to settle for anything less?

Secret #63: Expect the Best, Plan for the Worst

Expect the best. Prepare for the worst. Capitalize on what comes.
—Zig Ziglar

In order to accomplish all that we do, superachievers have complex plans to obtain our goals. We expect that the initial plans will go well; however, we always have multiple contingency plans for getting to the end goal. In other words, superachievers are really good at worst-case-scenario planning.

When planning how to achieve a goal (for example, starting a small business), the first step in the process is to set a basic plan (expecting the best results). Expecting the best results means to plan that I will have a certain amount of money in the bank to fund the business until the first big client is obtained, which will be within six months from the launch. Also, I will expect to have a certain amount of business expenses in obtaining this client, and so on.

Obviously there is much more involved in the initial planning stages, but you get the point. The next stage of planning involves what could go wrong (planning for the worst). The superachiever goes through the plan, and at each step in the process, assumes some sort of failure. What if the business launch is delayed? What if there isn't enough money in the bank to fund the first six months? What if it takes more than six months to sign up the first client? What if I don't see a paycheck for a year? The superachiever then creates miniplans for each of these possible contingencies.

By expecting the worst and planning for the best, the superachiever is easily able to implement a plan B, C, D, or E, in the event that they become necessary. This way, precious energy and time are not wasted by freaking out and then struggling to implement an emergency plan when the inevitable *shit happens*. Superachievers already have an emergency plan in place.

Reflections

1. What is your process for creating a plan with a goal you've chosen to accomplish?

2. How do you plan for the worst?

3. How has this process benefited you in the past and how will you incorporate it even more now?

Secret #64: Fun Is a Necessary Part of the Equation

We're so engaged in doing things to achieve purposes of outer value that we forget the inner value, the rapture that is associated with being alive, is what it is all about.

—Joseph Campbell

Superachievers are busy changing our lives, the lives of others, and ultimately the world, for the better. This is a serious mission with lots of responsibility, but it doesn't mean that it can't also be fun. Fun brings enjoyment and lighthearted amusement to the process, motivating the superachiever to work hard and achieve even more.

Some goals or dreams, which are necessary for the betterment of our world and ourselves, are tedious, require sacrifice, and are hard to accomplish. The superachievers know this and will do what we can to bring fun into the process, making it less arduous and even enjoyable.

How do superachievers accomplish this? It can be as simple as finding ways to make exercise fun so that the time passes more quickly during the process. It can also require a more complex effort, such as the several years I spent in violent-crime analysis. While working at the FBI's Violent Criminal Apprehension Program (ViCAP), it was my responsibility to help law enforcement agencies with their homicide, sexual assault, missing persons, and unidentified-human-remains cases. I knew this was an important mission and wanted to accomplish helping as many agencies and victims' families find closure as possible. The work could be emotionally draining, especially when I closely identified with the victims. I was able to bring some fun into the process by looking at the cases as puzzles to be solved, as well as turning it into a game of "catching the demented bad guy." By using this technique, I was able to be superproductive, literally work hundreds of cases, and be instrumental in getting several serial murderers and rapists off the streets.

Reflections

1. How have you brought fun into arduous or daunting tasks in the past?

2. Why is fun an important part of the equation to you?

3. How can you bring more fun into the achievement process?

Secret #65: Become an Options Expert

We have more possibilities in each moment than we realize.
—Thich Nhat Hanh

Superachievers know there are always options. You won't hear a superachiever saying, "I had no choice; I had to do it." We never feel like we've been backed into a corner and that there is no way out, because there is always a choice.

Understanding that there is always a choice is a state of mind. Superachievers are keenly aware that our childhoods or cultural and religious influences may affect this state of mind. For example, if a superachiever is raised in a culture or religion that deeply frowns on divorce and becomes "stuck" in an unhappy marriage, he or she understands that are still choices: (1) divorce, or (2) remaining in the marriage to honor a belief system, but exploring a number of other options to find happiness. Whatever choice superachievers make, we understand that they were indeed choices, and we will both make the best of and take responsibility for the resulting consequences.

Being options experts means that whenever decision points present themselves, we are able to identify a number of paths. When paths are chosen, we take full responsibility for the consequences. For example, when I finally came to the decision point on whether I would stick it out with the government until retirement (security) or become a small-business owner (risky), I also knew that there were a number of "between" options (like working for the government *and* owning a small business, etc.). I chose to leave and have gladly dealt with the consequences of forfeiting a retirement, taking a hit on my credit, and not having the same level of income (yet), because I know in the long term it will pay off financially, emotionally, and mentally to be living my dream.

Reflections

1. How are you able to identify multiple options for each decision point that presents itself to you?

2. How has being an options expert benefited you in the past?

3. How can you become even more of an options expert?

Secret #66: I Can Do It!
(Whatever It Is)

Don't limit yourself. Many people limit themselves to what they think they can do. You can go as far as your mind lets you. What you believe, remember, you can achieve.

—Mary Kay Ash

Superachievers have a belief that no matter what comes our way, no matter what goals we have set, we can do it. It will be accomplished. If we don't currently know how to do it (whatever it is), we firmly believe that we can learn how to do it.

This is not a delusional belief—if superachievers set their minds to become top surgeons in the medical field, they understand that it could potentially take twenty years to accomplish. This unwavering belief in oneself is foundational to being a superachiever. To believe that you are able to accomplish anything as well as handle anything that comes your way is incredibly freeing. It removes all the *stuff* that average folks have to deal with, such as doubt and fear, that can weigh you down and keep you from soaring into your dreams.

There are a number of times in my life that I have jumped into a project or position that I didn't know much about, but I was confident that I could learn as I progressed. I didn't allow the "not knowing" to stop me from taking advantage of the opportunity when it presented itself. Perhaps the biggest jump into the unknown I have taken is launching a small business. Prior to become a small-business owner, I had spent my entire career in government and was completely unfamiliar with the private sector and pretty much everything related to running a business. (I didn't consider the lemonade stand at age ten and other various endeavors as proper preparation.) This didn't stop me—I created my own crash course on small-business ownership, investing lots and lots of time in educating myself on best practices. This "I can do it" state of mind has allowed me to not only launch a business but also launch it quickly and successfully, and now I coach and teach others how to do the same.

Reflections

1. Do you have the belief that, no matter what it is, "I can do it"? Examine your past behavior—do you really hold this belief?

2. How has this belief helped you in the past?

3. How can you amplify this belief even more to help you take advantage of the opportunities that come your way?

Secret #67: Ride the Waves like a True Surfer

You can't stop the waves, but you can learn to surf.

—Unknown

Superachievers are surfers of life. We ride the waves, from the small ones to the big gnarly ones, and we even look "totally rad" while doing it. Sometimes we get kicked off our surfboards, but we get right back on. There are times we have to momentarily avert the ride—maybe a shark was spotted nearby—but we get back on the waves as soon as the waters are clear.

No matter what comes our way, superachievers are ready to handle it. We have an intuitive sense that regardless of what happens in our lives, we will find a way to come out on top. We enjoy life when the waters are calm, and when the big gnarly waves come, we rise up to the challenge like true surfers.

There was a five-year period in my early thirties when the big gnarly waves seemed like they would never quit crashing down, and the sharks were circling, waiting for me to fall off my metaphorical board. My dad passed away after a five-year battle with pancreatic cancer. I finally decided that life was too short to be married to someone I couldn't be myself around. Very soon after, I found myself as a single mom often battling my ex and his new girlfriend over seemingly trivial things. And to top it off, I got the worst boss that I have ever had in my entire life.

There were times when I felt like I was close to falling off the board and drowning, including one point when I had to spend a night in the hospital because my doctor thought I was having a stroke. During that time period, my main goal was to make it through the day (emotionally, mentally, and physically) while also creating a loving and comfortable environment for my two children. When the waves finally became a bit smaller, I was able to start focusing on some of my bigger goals, such as going back to school for another graduate degree to prepare for moving into the professional development field.

Reflections

1. Looking back at your life, what kinds of waves have you had to surf?

2. When you face the big gnarly waves, how quickly are you able to get back up on the board when you're knocked off?

3. How can you learn to surf a little better before the next set of big waves hits?

Secret #68: Conduct a Gap Analysis

Your vision of where or who you want to be is your greatest asset.
—Paul Arden

What exactly is a gap analysis? It is measuring where you currently are in life, determining where you want to be after a certain time period, and then figuring out how to get from point A to point B. Most superachievers love to make lists, charts, graphs, or some other organizational tool to conduct gap analyses of our lives. I've even seen mind maps to help make this process happen.

When doing a gap analysis, I generally use one-year increments for small goals, five-year increments for large goals, and ten-year increments for the *big hairy* goals (a.k.a. dreams). I recently did my five-year plan, so I can use that as an example. I looked at who I wanted to be in five years and decided that in 2020:

- I will have published at least two books.
- I will speak to large audiences (1000 plus) regularly.
- My business with my business partner will be turning a very nice profit, much of it through passive income.
- I will have completed at least one bucket-list travel adventure (such as going to Iceland to see the northern lights or drinking wine in Italy).
- I will finally get back down to the weight I was in high school.

These goals are then fleshed out into specific tasks with due dates to make them happen. I am happy to report that I am already close to achieving a couple of these before the five-year period is scheduled to start in January 2016 (would you expect anything less from a superachiever?).

Reflections

1. How often are you conducting a gap analysis on what you'd like to achieve and who you want to be?

2. Who do you want to be in one year? Five years? Ten years?

3. What are you going to do to get there?

Secret #69: Engage in Systems Thinking

In every aspect of life, have a game plan, and then do your best to achieve it.

—Alan Kulwicki

"Systems thinking" is a term often used in organizations when they are trying to figure out complex problems. It involves looking at the various parts of a system, how they are interrelated, and then looking at the system as a whole. It is a holistic approach to problem solving because it takes into consideration how, when one part of the system is changed, it will affect the other parts of the system. For example, if a specific customer-service policy is implemented in the customer-service department, the strategic team considers how it will affect sales, marketing, production, the leadership team, and the organization as a whole.

Superachievers adapt this systems-thinking approach to our lives and choices we make along our journeys of achievement. Systems thinking can be used, regardless of whether you need to make a small, seemingly inconsequential choice, or a big, hairy life-changing decision. What does this process look like? Quite simply, if you have set a goal of losing weight, you understand that eating a cookie that you really, really want may be inconsequential in the totality of the weight-loss journey, but giving into the temptation will keep you further from your goal than if you didn't eat it.

Utilizing systems thinking for big decisions gets much more complex, but it's the same as looking at how the process of achieving and the actual achievement of a goal will affect the different parts of your "system." For example, when I made the decision to leave a secure government position for the world of small-business ownership, I had to look at how it would affect my husband, my children, my mother and myself. I took it even deeper and looked at the potential financial, emotional, mental, and physical effects on each involved party, both short and long term.

Reflections

1. How do you engage in systems thinking for the seemingly inconsequential decisions you make?

2. How do you engage in systems thinking for the big, hairy life-changing decisions you make?

3. How can you better utilize systems thinking?

Secret #70: Call an Intervention

Ask for help not because you are weak, but because you want to remain strong.

—Les Brown

Superachievers are highly self-aware individuals. We know our strengths, we know our weaknesses, and we are keenly aware of when our strengths can become our weakness. This amazing level of self-awareness allows us to call an intervention when necessary.

Calling an intervention means bringing in help from others to get you back on course. Ultimately, it means asking for help, which is something your average person is not willing to do. Superachievers, however, know that there are times when we need help getting past a particular obstacle (most often, ourselves) in order to maximize our achieving potential.

What does calling an intervention look like? The first type of intervention can be set up before superachievers find themselves stuck. For example, I have a tendency, when really focused on a particular achievement, to get obsessive. So much so that I spend pretty much every moment of the day (even in my dreams) either working on or thinking about a particular goal and the process of achieving it. This can be a strength, to a point—until it leads to ignoring my mental, emotional, or physical needs (which isn't fun for anyone in my company). I have an agreement with those closest to me to intervene if they see me starting to go down that rabbit hole.

A second type of intervention is for superachievers to call in reinforcements when we are stuck in moving toward goals. For example, when I was having trouble finding funding for my crime analysis unit, I called in the help of the investigations and narcotics divisions, and we were able to get a grant that would fund projects in all three units.

Reflections

1. What types of interventions have you had to call in the past?

2. What prearranged interventions do you have with others? If you don't have any, what will you set up?

3. How can you call in an intervention sooner when you feel stuck?

Secret #71: The Road Less Traveled

Do not go where the path may lead, go instead where there is no path and leave a trail.

—Ralph Waldo Emerson

Superachievers enjoy being unique. We like taking the roads less traveled; however, we do not want to make things even more difficult than they already are, so we take the paths of least resistance on those roads. Superachieving can be a very difficult road. Knowing this, superachievers will take whatever steps necessary to ease our journeys, giving us additional energy to accomplish even more.

When I started my first business, a personal coaching firm, I knew that I would need to do more than just personal coaching to make the kind of income I envisioned. Being a lifelong trainer, I decided I would include a number of professional development workshops and programs to bring in approximately 60 percent of the business's revenue. I then considered what type of programs I wanted to offer, and the investment of time I would need in order to develop the full extent of programs I envisioned. After determining the amount of time it would take to develop the company's reputation and the programs, I decided there had to be another path (of least resistance) with a bigger return on investment.

I began looking at what other companies were doing in the arena of professional development and found one company that not only fit my philosophies perfectly but also had over twenty years of experience. They were offering franchise opportunities, so I gave them a call. After researching the company thoroughly, I invested in a franchise. I was able to take their professional development curriculum, as well as their reputation, and use it as a platform for my programs. This allowed me to come out of the proverbial gate running at full speed when the business was officially launched.

Reflections

1. Looking back at your experiences, how have you taken the road less traveled?

2. Looking back at your experiences, how have you taken the path of least resistance while still being different?

3. How can you turn up the volume on being different while still being effective and efficient?

Secret #72: Watch Out for "Cling-Ons"

Surround yourself with only people who are going to lift you higher. Life is already filled with those who want to bring you down.

—Oprah Winfrey

As discussed in previous secrets, there are several types of individuals that show up in a superachiever's life. Here are some categories I've identified:

- individuals who try to compete with the superachiever
- individuals who are jealous of superachievers' talents and will try to knock us down a peg or two so they can feel better about themselves
- individuals who appreciate the amazingness of superachievers, support us, and understand that we are a good asset to the team
- individuals who are attracted to the energy of the superachiever and siphon it with their negativity (energy vampires)

Finally, there are the individuals who recognize a good thing when they see it and want to catch a ride on the coattails of the superachiever while offering nothing in return. These individuals are considered to be "cling-ons" because they are able to sense that the superachiever is destined to accomplish great things, and they want to benefit from it in some way. Cling-ons are not to be confused with individuals who come to learn from the superachiever, such as a mentor/mentee, or even a champion-type relationship. Cling-ons simply want to benefit from the achievements of the superachiever or be associated with the reputation of a person *in the know*, who gets things done.

Like many superachievers, I've had my share of cling-ons. Sometimes it is hard to spot them, because we really do want to help others in their efforts at accomplishing their goals, and assuming malicious intent is not in our natures. It only took a couple of times of being taken advantage of for me to learn my lesson. Now I look at each relationship I enter into—business, coaching, mentoring, and so on, and ask myself if it is a mutually beneficial relationship. Am I better with them or without them? The benefit may simply be the satisfaction in helping another person who is grateful for assistance (which is a big benefit in my book), but the fundamental idea is that there needs to be some sort of mutual benefit.

Reflections

1. Reflect on your experiences with cling-ons in the past. How were you able to identify someone as a cling-on?

2. How do you feel about cling-ons?

3. How can you increase your awareness of cling-ons?

Secret #73: The Past Is the Past

Learn from the past and let it go. Live in today.

—Louise L. Hay

As humans, we are constantly living in the past because that is simply how our brains function. Think of the brain as a computer, logging every experience we have. As each new experience presents itself in our lives, our brains will search through the stored catalog of experiences and find a similar one. If we don't interrupt the process somehow, it will encourage the same reaction to the new experience, saving time and energy on coming up with a new response.

Superachievers intuitively understand how this process works and will stop and think before going into pure reaction mode. This understanding is vital and is often why superachievers do not allow past failures to freeze us in our tracks or bad experiences to keep us from moving forward in our lives. We know that the past is the past, and today is a new day. We also understand that we are who we are today because of all of our past experiences and are grateful for both the good and the bad.

What does this look like? There are many different examples that come to mind. The most prominent, which I venture to guess is something that many people in the United States struggle with, is the process of losing weight. Since adulthood, I have struggled with maintaining my ideal weight. Being an athlete during my preteen and teen years, I could eat whatever I wanted and even needed the extra calories. The eating habits I developed during those years did not serve me well when I became an adult.

My attempts at dieting over the years have failed more than they have succeeded; however, that has not stopped me from finding different ways to achieve the goals I set for myself. I put the failures in the past, consider them learning points on what doesn't work for me, and then move on to the next process to get to my goal. Interestingly, I finally decided to go to a medical doctor who specializes in weight loss, and have found much success, moving toward my goal more quickly than I had ever imagined. Sometimes the "long way" gets you to your goal the quickest, and the "shortcut" doesn't work.

Reflections

1. How have you been able to leave the past in the past?

2. Knowing how the brain works, what do you do to get yourself out of the automatic reaction it creates?

3. How can you be even more conscious of when the past is negatively impacting your current choice of actions?

Secret #74: Forgive Yourself and Others

When you forgive, you in no way change the past—but you do change the future.

—Bernard Meltzer

As presented in some of the other secrets, superachievers can be hardest on ourselves, more so than anyone else could ever be. Sometimes we forget that we are human and prone to all things human, including messing up. We hold ourselves to a higher standard and can become very upset with ourselves if we do not meet that standard.

Because we are so focused on our development, we also grow at an exponential rate—the people we are today are not the people we were yesterday, last year, five years ago, and so on. I look back on some of the things I've said and done in the past and am momentarily embarrassed that I would behave in that manner. But, being a superachiever, I know that self-forgiveness is crucial in not dwelling on past failures. By forgiving myself, I am able to free the mental energy and negativity wrapped up in the dwelling process and repurpose it to help me achieve the next goal.

Superachievers know that we also need to forgive others, although we usually find this easier than forgiving ourselves. This has been particularly hard for me in a number of situations, especially when I felt betrayed by the individual or felt that I did nothing to deserve his or her malicious intent.

However, as a superachiever, I know that forgiveness is not for other people—it is for me. It doesn't absolve them of their behaviors; rather, it allows me to move on. I can then use the mental energy I would be wasting on them to help move forward toward my goals.

Reflections

1. How good are you at forgiving yourself and others? Please explain.

2. How can you forgive yourself easier?

3. How can you forgive others easier?

Secret #75: Listen to Your Body

Our bodies communicate to us clearly and specifically, if we are willing to listen to them.

—Skakti Gawain

The body is an amazing instrument in indicating how well you are doing mentally, emotionally, and physically. It reflects back to its owner how his or her thoughts are manifesting in the body. Superachievers are very aware of the body's amazing ability to communicate what is going on, and we check in regularly to determine if we need to change our current course of action (unless, of course, we are due for an intervention—Secret #70).

Your state of mind is reflected in your body, sometimes instantly, depending on the strength of the thought or emotion. I have learned to monitor both my emotions and my energy levels, as those are the initial "tells" that there is something I need to examine further. For example, if I feel anger bubbling up via a tightening in my chest and throat during a conversation with someone, I realize that I've just been triggered. Before reacting, I need to examine what is behind that feeling.

If my energy levels are high, I know that I am taking care of my body, eating right, and moving in the right direction. If I feel low energy, I start to look at how I've been treating my body, as well as if I am feeling stuck. If, after making a decision on a project or in working with someone, I get a stomachache or feel a tightening in my throat, I know that my body is trying to tell me to examine the situation further—it is probably something I don't want to do. Thousands of years of evolution have given us some amazing sensing abilities that the brain doesn't always put into words such as "danger, danger!" or "doing well; keep up the good work," so it is important we listen to the body's response and search for further information.

Reflections

1. What do your varying energy levels tell you?

2. What types of reactions do you have in your body that tell you to examine something further?

3. How can you listen to your body more effectively?

Secret #76: Emotions Are Data

If your emotional abilities aren't in hand, if you don't have self-awareness, if you are not able to manage your distressing emotions, if you can't have empathy and have effective relationships, then no matter how smart you are, you are not going to get very far.

—Daniel Goleman

Superachievers are emotionally intelligent—we emote when we need to. However, we do not allow our emotions to control us. We understand that our emotions are simply data, bringing our attention to what we need to know.

It is important that you acknowledge your emotions, allow yourself to feel them, and then let them go. When we hold on to our emotions and allow ourselves to drown in them, that's when they become problematic for us. Our thoughts (consciously or subconsciously) create our emotions. Our emotions, in turn, affect our bodies. By holding on to our emotions or repressing them, we are negatively impacting the wellness of our bodies. For every psychological process, there is a physiological response. You could literally be making yourself sick if you aren't allowing yourself to process your emotions in a healthy manner.

Superachievers acknowledge and feel our emotions. We examine what messages are being sent to us, and then let the emotions go. For example, you observe someone roll his or her eyes while you're speaking in a meeting. You feel the anger start to bubble up—rather than letting it fester and allow resentment for the other person to take over, you acknowledge to yourself, "Wow! I took that personally!" Then you let it go.

Superachievers have too much to accomplish to allow wasted energy on emotional drama; like everything else, they process quickly.

Reflections

1. What emotions are you still holding onto?

2. How do you process your emotions?

3. Think of a recent time you felt a strong emotion. What was the message in it?

Secret #77: Enjoy the Journey!

Focus on the journey, not the destination. Joy is found not in finishing an activity, but in doing it.

—Greg Anderson

This is the biggest secret known to superachievers that others often misunderstand. Others will watch the superachievers' constant successes and believe that we live for putting the next trophy on our shelves, or the additional money in the bank from our promotions, or the latest achievements on our resumes. Sure, those things are nice, and it does feel really great to accomplish something, but this isn't why we do it. Most superachievers could care less if we get recognized for our accomplishments; we know it is par for the course.

Instead, superachievers are all about the *journey.* The *process* of achieving is what drives us. We find great satisfaction in tackling whatever challenges we decide to take on. We are in awe of how we must continually grow in order to achieve what we want, that we must literally become the people who are able to meet the next challenges. I can't remember where I got this, but I keep it on a sticky note on my desk: "Who you are now is not who you will be when you accomplish your goals." This is what drives a superachiever—*constant growth.*

We only get so many trips around the sun in our lifetimes. The ultimate goal of the superachiever is to make the most of each of these trips—to pack in as much living as possible with what time we have on this earth. We want those little dashes between the years of our births and our deaths on our headstones to represent lives well lived. We want lives in which we loved ourselves and others to their fullest. Most of all, we want lives in which we didn't let anything stop us from living out our dreams and becoming the people we were meant to be. We hope that we left this world a little better than we found it.

Reflections

1. How has your journey been so far?

2. How can you make your journey even more fabulous?

3. Quit [bleeping] around, and get to it!

Final Thoughts

It's time to show up fully—to embrace who you are and unleash your superachiever awesomeness to help make this world a better place.

—Christina M. Eanes

It is my sincere hope that you were able to relate to these seventy-seven secrets to superachieving as well as use them to motivate you to step into your awesomeness even more. There are many of us superachievers out there, lying dormant, tired of the struggle of being ourselves in a world that supports being average.

This book is a call to action for you to step into your greatness. As Marianne Williamson stated, "Our deepest fear is that we are powerful beyond measure. It is our light, not our darkness, that most frightens us." You are a powerful being, and it is time to let your light shine fully. The world needs you, and you can no longer hang out on the sidelines—it's time to not only jump into the game, but also to take the lead.

Here is your call to action: Think of the biggest, most bodacious dream you can fathom. Go do it!

Challenge accepted?

Reflections

1. What three secrets have you absolutely mastered? How will you use them to benefit you even more?

2. What three secrets surprised you as being related to superachieving? Why?

3. What three secrets do you need to work on the most? What is your improvement plan?

About the Author

Christina M. Eanes, a lifelong superachiever, is on a mission to help others embrace their own inner superachiever. She holds a BS and an MS in criminal justice leadership, as well as an MS in education with a specialization in training and performance improvement, and she is a Certified Professional Co-Active Coach (CPCC).

Through more than fifteen years of public service with a California police department and the Federal Bureau of Investigation (FBI), Christina worked on an array of programs, including the FBI's Violent Criminal Apprehension Program and the FBI's Leadership Development Program, where she helped train thousands of leaders.

After advancing to a senior manager position within the FBI before turning forty, Christina decided to open her own business to help people transform their personal and professional lives.

She has two amazing children (now young adults) and currently lives in Washington, DC, with her wonderfully supportive husband and four adorable cats.

For more information, visit www.quitbleepingaround.com

Made in the USA
Middletown, DE
26 February 2017